Parent Talk

How to Talk to Your Children in Language That Builds Self-Esteem and Encourages Responsibility

Chick Moorman

A Fireside Book
Published by Simon & Schuster
New York   London   Toronto   Sydney

FIRESIDE
Rockefeller Center
1230 Avenue of the Americas
New York, NY 10020

FIRESIDE and colophon are registered trademarks
of Simon & Schuster, Inc.

For information regarding special discounts for bulk purchases,
please contact Simon & Schuster Special Sales at
1-800-456-6798 or business@simonandschuster.com

Designed by William Ruoto

Manufactured in the United States of America

5   7   9   10   8   6   4

Library of Congress Cataloging-in-Publication Data
Moorman, Chick.
Parent talk: how to talk to your children in language that builds self-
esteem and encourages responsibility / Chick Moorman.
p. cm.
Originally published: Merrill, Mich. : Personal Power Press, 1998.
1. Parent and child. 2. Parenting. 3. Child rearing. 4. Communication in
the family. 5. Self-esteem in children. 6. Responsibility in children.
I. Title.
HQ755.85.M653   2003
649'.1—dc21   2002036544

ISBN-13: 978-0-7432-3624-9
ISBN-10:   0-7432-3624-6

In loving memory of Randal Paul Moorman
September 13, 1967–July 8, 1997

Acknowledgments

I wish to thank several people who enabled me to write this book. Nancy Lewis invested hours of her time reading this manuscript and making helpful suggestions. Her editing skills and background as an English teacher, writer, and editor added immensely to the book you now hold in your hands. Her listening skills, empathy, and deep concern for me and this project helped me remain sane and centered throughout the writing process. Her expertise and commitment were highly needed and appreciated.

Martha Campbell is responsible for all the cartoons you see in this book. Her talent, creativity, and sense of humor have added a much-needed touch of "lighten up" to this project.

I honor Debbie Dukarski, my former office manager and friend, for her encouragement, assistance, and persistence. Not only did she use these ideas with her daughter, she dragged me kicking and screaming into the twenty-first century by insisting that I buy a computer/word processor. As usual, Debbie was correct. It is easier to write on a word processor than to use paper, pencil, and eraser.

Thank you to Peggy Lange, who typed all these words more than once. Peggy's computer wizardry has helped immensely with this book and with my mailings and workshop materials.

I appreciate and honor Nancy Weber, who initially thought up the teacher talk/parent talk concept and first used it in a workshop with professional educators. Many of her original ideas appear on these pages with adaptation. Her ideas and thoughts make up a good portion of this book.

To all the parents who attended my parent trainings and beseeched me to put these ideas together, thank you for the encouragement and for keeping up the pressure. It is finished. And I love it. I believe you will, too.

Enjoy.

—Chick Moorman

Contents

Acknowledgments   VII
Introduction   XVII

Choices
"Do you want your eggs fried or scrambled?"   2
"Choose. Decide. Pick."   5
Cartoon   9
"You always have more choices than you think you have."
    10
"Please make a different choice."   12
Cartoon   15
"Please make a decision."   16
"You decide."   19
"Don't be a quitter."   22

Response-ability
"Act as if . . ."   26
"You're a car."   29
"Check yourself."   32

"Check it out inside."   34

"What's your goal?"   36

Cartoon   39

"Make a picture in your mind."   40

"Soon I'll be gone."   45

"What do you attribute that to?"   48

"I'm willing to pay part of it."   52

Cartoon   55

"No."   56

"You sure are persistent."   59

"Determination."   64

"You always/never . . ."   67

"It's easy."   70

"This is going to be hard."   73

"That's impossible."   75

The Search for Solutions

"Sounds like you have a problem."   80

"I know you can handle it."   83

"Every problem has a solution."   85

Cartoon   88

"I want you to help me solve my problem."   89

"We've got a problem. Who's willing to help?"   93

Learned Helplessness

*Ten Things to Say to Promote Learned Helplessness in Your
     Children*   98

"Here, let me do that."   99

"You sure are lucky."   102

"One . . . two . . . three . . ."   104

Cartoon   106

"There you go again."   107

"That's the fifth time I've had to speak to you about this."
     109

"That's not a good excuse."   111

Cartoon   114

"Be careful or you'll spill that."   115

Praise, Criticism, and Self-Esteem

"You did a good job."   120

"All your letters are right between the lines."   123

"I appreciate your efforts. Thanks."   126

Ten Things to Say to Share Appreciation   128

"That's terrible."   129

"Next time . . ."   132

Parent Talk at Its Worst

The Twenty Worst Things to Say to Your Child   136

"If you don't straighten up, I'm going to leave you here."
    137
"Why can't you be more like your sister?"   139
"I was only teasing."   141
"Act your age."   143
"What did I just tell you?"   145
Fifteen Things Parents Say to Guilt-trip Their Children   147
"We never wanted you anyway."   150

Intimacy

Ten Things to Say to Build Family Solidarity   154
Cartoon   155
"I love you."   156
"Sally, Charles, Roberto, Mary, Helene . . ."   159
"I noticed."   161
"Different people have different needs."   164
"Inch by inch."   166
"Some of us . . ."   168
"I'm sorry."   170
"Touch each other gently."   172
The Ten Best Things You Can Say to Your Children
    174
Twenty Ways to Say "I Love You" to Your Children
    175

Feelings

Seven Things to Say to Help Your Child Feel Heard   178

"Sounds like you're feeling frustrated."   180

"That's nothing to feel bad about!"   183

"I understand just how you feel."   185

"You can show me how you're feeling with this pillow."   188

"Don't you talk to me like that!"   190

"If I were you . . ."   193

"Say you're sorry."   197

Cartoon   200

Increasing Conflict

Ten Things to Say to Increase Conflict   202

"Because I said so, that's why."   203

Cartoon   206

"Okay, who did it?"   207

"Tell me your side of it."   209

"Did you win?"   211

"Why did you do that?"   214

"I told you so."   216

Reducing Conflict

Ten Things to Say to Reduce Conflict   220

"I see clothes on the floor." 221

"I don't like what I just heard. If you're angry, tell me
  another way." 224

Cartoon 226

"How can we see this differently?" 227

"I'm tired of seeing you behave this way." 230

"How can you both get what you want?" 233

Cartoon 236

"Wouldn't it?" 237

"You're probably right." 240

"Stop whining." 243

"Is that a real fight or are you just faking it?" 247

"What did you really want to tell her?" 249

"We'll see." 252

"My patience is running out." 254

"I don't want to hear any more tattling!" 256

Odds and Ends

"I'm proud for you." 260

"Chad, your coat is on the floor. I'm getting angry. It belongs
  on a hanger in the closet." 262

"Luis, as you hang up your coat, please straighten the boots in
  the closet." 265

"I'll take you to the mall when your room is clean."
  267

Cartoon 269

"What <u>will</u> you do?" 270

"I love you, and I don't like that behavior."   272

"I'm really surprised."   274

"It's homework time."   276

Cartoon   279

"I think I'll get started on my work. A fast start helps
  motivate me to keep going."   280

"Who do you want to be?"   283

"I love you."   286

Introduction

Your choice of words and your style of communication, are critical to the self-esteem, emotional health, and personal empowerment of your children. There is an undeniable link between the words you speak and your child's behaviors and attitudes. The way you talk to your children affects their perceptions, interpretations, beliefs, values, and approach to life; it influences their actions as well as the consequences of those actions. By carefully choosing and using words and phrases that build self-esteem and encourage self-responsibility, you can help your children become more capable, caring human beings. That's what Parent Talk, the skills-based program described in this book, is all about. It will teach you a series of verbal skills and language patterns to help you raise responsible, respectful children as you reduce stress, strain, and family conflict.

We often use words without thinking about their effect. We repeat certain phrases out of habit or use words that our parents once used with us. My hope is that *Parent Talk* will help you become more conscious of the words you use—and aware of the power you wield when you use words that praise, nurture, and empower as well as words that scold, shame, and criticize. In the pages that follow you'll recognize comments, suggestions, questions, and commands that I hear parents say to their children every day. Some I'll recommend you continue to use because they will help your children become more response-able (able to respond in healthy ways to all that life throws at them). Others I'll ask you to eliminate from your parent talk repertoire because they encourage learned helplessness, power struggles, and mutual resentment. I realize it's not easy to break ingrained habits, so whenever I suggest you stop using a particular phrase, I'll suggest emotionally healthy alternatives.

The first chapter, "Choices," will help you learn to construct language that offers age-appropriate, controlled choices to your children. You will also learn to use language that helps children become conscious of the choices they express through their words and actions.

"Response-ability," the second chapter, is an effort to help you assist your children to become more response-able—as I wrote above, able to perceive and make a variety of healthy responses to the situation at hand. It includes the "I can't" antidote, language that will encourage children to develop a strong inner authority, and attribute-awareness strategies that help children understand how their choice of words and deeds can have both positive and negative consequences.

"The Search for Solutions" focuses on parent talk that encourages a solution-seeking mindset in children. The foundation is language that communicates your belief in your children's ability to solve many of their own problems.

I wrote the chapter "Learned Helplessness" for parents who tend to "overfunction." In other words, parents who tend to do so much for their children that their children don't learn to do much of anything for themselves. This chapter will help you stamp out learned helplessness in your family and create autonomous, independent children who can think and act for themselves in emotionally, mentally, and physically healthy ways.

"Praise, Criticism, and Self-Esteem" warns against the excessive use of evaluative praise, the style of praise that creates praise junkies. Being hooked on praise may not sound life threatening, but the sad truth is that praise junkies don't have a genuine sense of their own self-worth. Instead they're on an endless chase after external proof of it. The far healthier alternative is descriptive and appreciative praise that encourages a strong internal sense of self-esteem, an esteem that comes from the inside out rather than from the outside in.

"Parent Talk at Its Worst" reminds us all that children are abused with words far more often than with fist or belt. Words wound. The physical bruises and scars they create aren't immediately evident, but instead show up later as defiance, delinquency, addiction, learning disabilities, and negative attitudes.

"Intimacy" and "Feelings" discuss ways to bond with your children, creating a strong sense of belonging. You can use the skills presented here to build family solidarity as well as help your children feel that they are being heard. Specifically, this chapter addresses how to respond effectively to a child caught up in strong emotion.

"Increasing Conflict" and "Reducing Conflict" each offer language patterns to avoid as well as those to put into practice if reducing family conflict is on your parenting wish list. These skills, coupled with those presented in "The Search for Solutions," will reveal the silver lining in conflicts. Conflicts can be constructive and resolved in ways that meet the needs of both parent and child.

"Odds and Ends" is a collection of the remaining Parent Talk tools. Here you will learn to separate the deed from the doer, communicate strong feeling without wounding the spirit, and make self-referred comments (statements about your own behavior with a family value attached) to influence your child's behavior.

In the pages that follow you'll read quite a bit about raising response-able children, and my hope is that along the way you'll become more response-able parents. By increasing the number of tools you have in your parenting tool box, you increase the likelihood that you will match the most effective tool to the appropriate situation. It is often said that if the only tool you have is a hammer, you tend to look at everything as if it were a nail. Sometimes a hammer is just what's called for. Other times, it's a screwdriver, chisel, wrench, or drill. With a variety of tools from which to choose, you no longer have to rely on a hammer when what you really need is a drill. When you can pick and choose from several Parent Talk skills, you have become a more response-able parent.

But the truth is, having tools isn't enough. To become an effective parent, you have to put the tools you have at your disposal to use. Regularly. People do not become good drivers, golfers, skiers, or horseback riders overnight. It takes much practice under a variety of conditions to become proficient at these endeavors. The same holds true for Parent Talk skills. Put simply, the skills work if you work the skills.

Between the covers of this book are hundreds of pages of what I've learned as a parent, a grandparent, and an educator. But my intent is not to overwhelm you with ideas. It is to offer you a variety from which to choose. The best way to begin is to begin simply. I suggest you start with two or three Parent Talk phrases. Write your selected phrases on note cards and carry them around with you. Tape them on your refrigerator or your bathroom mirror. Display them on the dashboard of your car. They're there to remind you of your goal to integrate this new language into everyday conversations with your kids.

When you're reminded of a Parent Talk phrase, see if you can put it to use immediately. See how many times you can use it in the next thirty minutes. Go ahead, exaggerate it. Play with it. Use these new skills whenever you can. Eventually, if you persist, you will hear yourself using this new repertoire effortlessly. When you get to that point, congratulate yourself. This is exactly where you want to be. When a phrase becomes second nature, it's a sign that you have successfully integrated it into your Parent Talk tool kit. The next step? Focus on a new phrase. Choose other pieces of the Parent Talk System and begin the process again. I think you'll start to notice positive change in the tone and spirit of the talk around your dinner table.

I promise you there is no single Parent Talk word or phrase that spoken once will immediately transform your parenting style or your child. This book teaches a system of communicating, a way of speaking, a style of language that with consistent use will have a cumulative effect. Repetition is the key. Repeated use of these words and phrases, delivered with an open heart, will eventually transform your relationship with your children.

There is no one best place to begin implementing the Parent Talk System. You could start with the first phrase in this book or the last. There is no prescribed order to follow. As you read through these pages, simply look for phrases that resonate with you. Focus on those that fit with your parenting philosophy and family values. You will know where you need to begin. Trust that you know. Begin at *your* beginning. Let the rest of your steps flow from there. Your children will let you know by their behavior what steps you need to take next.

Workshop participants often tell me they feel guilty after reading *Parent Talk*. "I wish I had known and used more of this material when my children were younger," they say. I tell them, "I wish I had known and used more of this material when my children were younger, too." And I mean it. Then I remind myself that what I knew at the time is what I knew at the time. There is no way I could have implemented skills that were not part of my parenting tool box. The same is true for you.

My intention is not to encourage you to feel guilt or remorse over words you have used in the past, but rather to provide you with new perspectives on old patterns of communication, along with an array of new choices. My hope is that you'll use *Parent Talk* to become more aware of your word choices and the effect they have on your children. Use it as a resource to strengthen communication with your youngsters, starting today.

When I wrote *Parent Talk*, my children were grown. Two of them had children of their own. I was traveling all over the country, lecturing and teaching seminars on how to raise responsible, caring, confident youngsters. I was speaking, writing, dancing, riding horses, and enjoying the single life. And, truthfully, using the skills I had written about only occasionally with my grandchildren and my grown children.

Then it happened. Overnight, with no warning, my life was turned upside down. My oldest daughter, Marti, died unexpectedly. Her children, Chelsea, age fourteen, and Austin, age eleven, moved in with me. Although I had wonderful support from relatives, the primary responsibility of raising these two children was suddenly mine.

One day I was at home alone, thinking mostly about myself. The next day I was the head of a family that included two adolescents.

A year later, I feel deeply blessed. There is more love in my home now than in the past nine years. If I could, I would change the circumstances that brought these two incredible children into my life full time. Yet I would not want to give up the love and affection that are now a part of my daily life. Softball games, volleyball games, sibling rivalry, school conferences, tae kwon do, the testing of limits. It seems like I've been here before.

I have learned some important parenting lessons in the past year. First, I learned it's a lot easier to travel all around the country telling other people how to raise children than it is to do it. There is always a gap between theory and practice. Practicing what you preach isn't always easy.

Most important, I relearned that the skills work if you work the skills. The Parent Talk strategies presented in this book are not pie-in-the-sky theories that only sound good on paper. They really do work if you use them—and use them, and use them.

When I am in my higher self, when I am on my game, when I am feeling good and using the skills consistently, things go well here. Peace reigns. Conflict is worked out to the benefit of all. Courtesy and respect are present. Parenting is fun, even when there are problems. I like myself better.

When I am not on my game, when I forget to use the skills, I can always tell. It shows up behaviorally in the children and in myself. There is more bickering and sulking and self-isolation. The flavor and tenor of the whole house changes. Parenting is not fun. I don't like myself as much.

I can tell you this: The hardest part for me now is remembering to use the skills, even though I know these skills inside out. I wrote the book! For me it is not a matter of knowing the skills. The issue is remembering to use them when I am tired, stressed, and angry. That is my challenge.

To meet that challenge, I have begun carrying note cards with me again, to remind myself of what I'm trying to do. My goal is to stay conscious, to remain aware of when I am using the skills and when I am not. When I become aware that I am not using Parent Talk skills I can choose again. When I am conscious, I have the choice. And my conscious choice is always to use the skills.

Today I am choosing to relearn and use these skills to create happy, caring, confident, response-able children. I invite you to join me.

Choices

"Do you want your eggs fried or scrambled?"

There is power in choice. The equation here is simple and direct. The more choices you have, the greater sense of personal power you experience. The less choice you have, the weaker your sense of personal power.

Whenever feasible, use parent talk that gives children choices. This increases their decision-making ability and gives them an opportunity to exercise the power that is available to them. As they perceive and act on the choices they have, their perception of themselves as able and empowered individuals increases.

"Do you want the sweater or the sweatshirt with the hood?"
"Do you prefer toast or an English muffin this morning?"
"Do you want to do the dishes now or after you call your friend?"

"Would you rather carry your coat or wear it?"
*"Would you prefer a party for six or have two friends
to sleep over?"*

Responsible behavior, decision-making ability, and feelings of power and control are directly related to the number of decisions children make. The more practice they get, the more skillful they become. More decisions equals more practice. More practice equals more skill. More skill equals more responsibility. More responsibility signals effective parenting.

Controlled choice is preferable to unlimited choice. When choices aren't limited, children often feel overwhelmed and have difficulty deciding. "You can have any cereal on the shelf" is an example of unlimited choice. *"Wheaties or Cheerios are the options for today"* reflects limited choice. Limited choice is an example of shared control in action. You have control because you control the number of choices. Your child has control because he gets to pick from the choices offered.

Children often want what is not a choice. In those cases, let your parent talk be calm and firm while you repeat the choices.

"Dad, I want a chocolate malt."
*"We're getting cones today, Bonnie. You can have chocolate,
vanilla, or twist."*
"I want a malt or a chocolate sundae."
"Chocolate, vanilla, or twist cone?"
"Please."

"Chocolate, vanilla, or twist cone?"
"Okay, I'll have chocolate."

Your child's ability to make choices begins with your decision to offer them. You can select parent talk that offers choices or not. It's your choice.

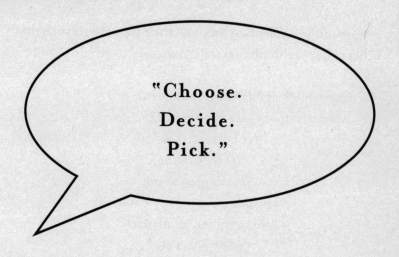

"Choose.
Decide.
Pick."

If you want to help your children see themselves as responsible for their own behavior, add these three special words, *choose, decide,* and *pick,* to your parent talk.

> "I noticed you *decided* to be fired
> up today."
> "How come you *picked* your grumpy mood?"
> "What response did you *choose* when the problems
> got tougher?"
> "How did you *decide* to act when your coach pulled
> you out of the game?"

Many children do not know that they pick how they act. They simply don't realize that they choose their own attitudes and behaviors. They firmly believe someone or something else is responsible for their actions, and their language reveals that belief. They say things like:

"*He* made me do it."
"*She* gave me a D."
"*He* hurt my feelings."
"*It's* frustrating."
"*That* depressed me."
"*My sister* changed my mind."
"*He* swept me off my feet."
"*Math* bores me."

Children often use language to blame an adult, a peer, a sibling, or some other external source for their own attitude or behavior. "That *teacher* bored me to death sixth hour," they complain, disowning any responsibility for the creation of their own boredom. "My *dad* made me do it over," they whine, giving up responsibility for the part they played in creating an inferior product in the first place. "*She* got me going," they respond, in an effort to blame a sister for their own outburst of giggling at the dinner table.

Choose, decide, and *pick* are words you can purposefully fit into your parent talk to put responsibility back on your child's shoulders. "*If you choose to leave your toys here, you'll be* choosing *to have them put on the shelf for a week*" communicates to your son that *you* are not responsible for whether or not he has his toys to play with next week. He is. "*If you* choose *to have your chores completed by two o'clock, I'll take you to the mall*" helps your daughter see that *she* is in control of going or not going to the mall. Other examples include:

"When you *decide* to return the car with the gas tank empty, you *choose* not to use the car during the following weekend."

"When you *pick* whining, I don't respond favorably."

"I got a call from the principal today. Apparently you *chose* an interesting response when the substitute teacher was there."

Repetitive use of the words *choose, decide,* and *pick* helps children appreciate that they do indeed choose. Repetition is a key. They don't understand the first few times. It takes many exposures to these words of self-responsibility before children really figure out that *you are not doing to them, they are choosing for themselves.*

Recently I witnessed the following scene in a sixth-grade classroom while the students were out for recess. In the middle of my conversation with the teacher, one of her students came in with a bloody nose. He cleaned himself up in the restroom and then approached the teacher. "Mrs. Whithelm, I just wanted to let you know I'll be going down to the principal's office. I'm not sure when I'll be back. I *chose* to get in a fight on the playground." When the young man left, I applauded the teacher because I knew of her effort to model and teach self-responsible language. She had used the three special words many times in her classroom.

I often tell this anecdote in teacher and parent workshops, but some adults don't understand its significance. "What's the big deal?" they question. "So what if he said, 'I chose'? The kid still got in a fight."

True, the student did choose to *fight.* Clearly there is more work to be done with this young man. Someone will need to spend time problem solving with him, creating a new plan of action for how he could choose to behave next time.

Don't miss the significance here. This sixth grader previously disowned all responsibility for his choices. "He *made me* do it," he would say, or "He *looked* at me." That language revealed he didn't see himself at choice. He was unconscious of his role in each encounter. In his mind it was always someone else's fault.

"I *chose* to get in a fight" represents a big change for this child. He's still choosing to fight, but at least he's conscious of the choice. Because this student now owns his actions, there is an increased chance he will make a more appropriate choice in the future.

Use *choose, decide,* and *pick* with your children. Incorporate these three special words into your language and enjoy the positive effects they have on your children's level of responsibility.

"MY PARENTS CALL IT CHOOSING TO SPEND THE EVENING WITH YOUR FAMILY. I CALL IT BEING GROUNDED."

"You always have more choices than you think you have."

Allison complained bitterly to her mother about not being able to afford the dress she wanted for the senior dance. Megan couldn't figure out how to fix her bicycle. Raul had no clear idea of how to improve his social studies grade. Each discussed their feelings of frustration with a parent. Although the situations were different, the parent response was the same. Each parent informed his or her child, *"You always have more choices than you think you have."*

Children don't always see the alternatives in their lives. Often, they focus on one solution and don't see beyond it. Their thinking becomes narrowed, and other possibilities cease to exist in their minds. The parent talk phrase *"You always have more choices than you think you have"* serves as a gentle reminder that thinking can be expanded and that more possibilities always exist.

If a child does not perceive a specific choice, then that alternative doesn't exist as a possible choice for him. To expand possibility thinking in your children and increase their range of options, use language that helps them tune in to the alternatives that do exist in their lives. Helpful variations include:

"What are some other possibilities here?"
"How else can you solve this?"
"What are other choices that you can consider?"
"What ways do you see of handling this?"
"How can you increase your list of alternatives?"
"What new choices have you thought of?"

As awareness of possible choices expands, problem-solving ability and feelings of competence increase along with it. Our children occasionally forget how powerful and competent they really are. During those times they just might appreciate the friendly reminder *You always have more choices than you think you have.*

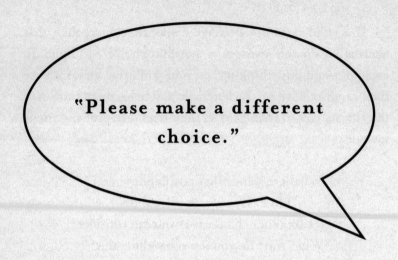

"Please make a different choice."

The assembly had already begun. Students sat on bleachers as teachers and administrators stood along the sides of the gym. The speaker, standing behind a podium, was well into his "Just Say No to Drugs" message when two students near the front began a conversation. Their actions were distracting to the presenter. He chose to ignore the behavior and continue his message, but the conversation didn't stop. It escalated into giggling and harsh whispers. Soon other students became distracted. Teachers began sending menacing glances in the direction of the culprits. The presenter continued to ignore the disruption, but the disturbance got louder. No one intervened. Finally, the speaker realized it was his responsibility to take some action.

What would you do if you were this speaker? What if you were one of the teachers present? How would you handle the situation?

The speaker considered several choices. He could continue without acknowledging the disturbance. He could move away from the podium and place himself in close proximity to the two disruptive students. He could tell them to "knock it off." Or he could end his speech and walk out.

This speaker made another choice. He paused and walked toward the students. Frowning, he looked at them and, very quietly, said, "I'm feeling distracted by your behavior. *Please make a different choice.*" He did not scold, reprimand, or hold them up to public ridicule. In fact, his conversation was low-key and private. Only the students on either side of the culprits were aware of what the speaker said. He simply let the disrupters know how their behavior was affecting him and suggested that they *"make a different choice."*

By telling these students to make a different choice, the speaker used language that communicated respect. His message informed them, "I see you as responsible for your own actions. You control your behavior. You choose your responses to life."

He didn't order them to "be quiet." He didn't threaten, "If you don't straighten up, you'll have to leave." He didn't even tell them *what* to do. By suggesting that the students make a different choice, the speaker communicated that he trusted they were intelligent enough to choose an appropriate response. His words left no doubt that he felt they needed to choose differently and he left the decision of how to respond to them. This communicated to the students that their actions affected him. It helped them understand that their behavior has impact.

Practice the phrase *"Make a different choice"* with your

children. When siblings are contemplating a fight, tell them, "We don't threaten with our fists here. *Make a different choice.*" "The rule is that we keep our shoes off the furniture. *Please make a different choice.*" When a child is cheating, say "You're choosing to go out of turn. That spoils the game for everyone. *Make a different choice.*" "That loud voice is distracting to me. *I want you to make a different choice*" is a respectful way to communicate your discomfort with the noise level.

Often when children are disruptive or behave inappropriately, parents attempt to change their behaviors by overpowering them with commands and orders. This tactic opposes an attitude of mutual respect and caring and is more likely to cause children to resist rather than change. *"Make a different choice"* shares some of the power with children and allows them responsibility for their own behavior. They are then more likely to respond appropriately by making a different choice.

"HER MOTHER TOLD HER TO QUIT BITING HER FINGERNAILS, BUT SHE MADE A DIFFERENT CHOICE."

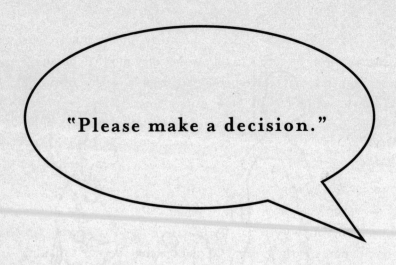

"*Please make a decision* to stay with us or to go to the time-out area."
"*Please make a decision* to follow the rules or to choose a different activity."
"*Please make a decision* to play quietly or to sit apart."

"*Please make a decision*" is strategic parent talk designed to put the ball of responsibility in the child's court. It asks a child to examine her behavior and take responsibility for changing it. It presents a choice that puts her in control of a portion of her life.

Most of the time children will choose the desirable behavior when asked to make a decision. They will choose to stay with the family, follow the rules, or play quietly. When they make these choices, it's important that their subsequent behaviors actually follow the choice.

If a child makes a decision to play quietly but shrieks instead, or if she agrees to follow the rules and then doesn't, I recommend that you choose language that describes the behavior and refers to the decision. *"I noticed that you didn't move back two spaces when the spinner directed you to. Your behavior shows me you've decided not to participate in the game."* *"When you yell during your brother's study time, you tell me you've decided to play in your room."*

When you choose parent talk that focuses on the child's decision, you stay clear of the persecutor role. Both parent and child more clearly understand that the child herself is making a decision to choose a consequence, that you're not arbitrarily deciding to punish her. As the days unfold and your language patterns contain many variations of "I see you've decided not to," the child more clearly understands cause and effect. Many children come to realize that it is they themselves who control whether or not the consequences are implemented. They loosen their hold on the perception of themselves as victims and learn to see themselves as co-creators of their own circumstances.

One variation of *"Please make a decision"* allows the child to decide when she is ready to resume the activity. Some examples are:

"When you decide you're ready, you may rejoin us at the dinner table."
"When you figure out what you'll do differently and put it in writing, we can discuss your using the car again."
"When you decide to follow the rules, you can ask Bill if he still wants to play the game."

This style of parent talk not only helps the child see that she is responsible for ending the activity but clarifies her role in resuming it.

You, the parent, are responsible for the discipline structure within your home. Your language can help children realize the choices and controls they have within that structure. As you continue to use the type of communication described in this book, your children will grow to understand that the choices they make impact what happens to them. They will gradually develop the internal controls necessary for independence and self-responsibility, both of which are ultimate goals of discipline.

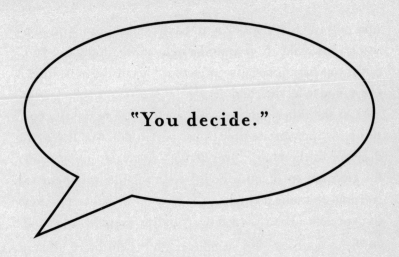

"You decide."

Many times throughout the day children ask questions that place the parent in a decision-making role.

"Can I have a snack?"
"Can I go outside to play?"
"Can I call Grandma?"

These common questions can be answered quickly and efficiently by the parent with a simple "yes" or "no," or they can be used to create numerous opportunities to empower children. Phrases like *you decide* can effectively place the decision-making responsibilities with the child. *"You decide"* frees the parent from the authoritarian role and helps the child get in touch with his personal power.

Use this style of parent talk only when your internal reaction is "yes." If it's not okay to have a snack, or if you don't want your child to go outside right now, simply say "no." Since you have a negative preference about the issue, this is not a time to let the child decide.

On the other hand, if your inclination is to say "yes," this is an appropriate time to use parent talk that leaves the decision to the child. *"You decide"* creates an opportunity for children to practice being decisive. It gives them the freedom to make a choice. It is one more chance for them to experience their own power and to exercise independence.

Add a condition to *"You decide"* to help children develop their decision-making ability.

"Can I watch television now?"
"If you can do it so it doesn't disturb others. You decide."

"Can I go outside to play?"
If you'll remember to come in when it starts raining. You decide."

"Can I call Grandma?"
"If you'll finish within the fifteen-minute limit. You decide."

When you qualify *"You decide"* by adding a condition, you give children criteria and require thinking. The condition gives them something concrete on which to base their decision. You help them develop their choice-making ability and their thinking skills simultaneously.

Other parent talk phases that work as well as *"You decide"* are:

"It's up to you."
"It's your choice."
"You choose."
"You can pick."
"You get to decide."
"You make that decision."
"I'm comfortable with whatever you decide."

Regardless of which phrase you choose, the stance towards children is one of respect. Although your words are "It's up to you" or "It's your choice," the real message you send is "I trust your judgment. You are capable of making many of your own decisions."

"Don't be a quitter."

"You can't quit."
"If you start it, you have to finish."
"Once you make a commitment, you need to stick to it."
"Once you start, you don't get to quit."

These parent talk examples are variations on the same theme. They are spoken by parents with the positive intention of informing children that quitting is an undesirable attribute. They want their children to finish what they start, keep their commitments, and follow through with the decisions they make.

While perseverance is an admirable trait and certainly worth encouraging in our children, the *"Don't be a quitter"* message often produces negative effects. Children who consistently are forced to keep their commitments in spite of their strong desire to quit learn that it's easier to not start something new than it is to get out of it. As a result, they don't often choose to begin new experiences.

A child who has been forced to complete six months of Girl Scouts after she figured out by the third meeting that she hated it isn't likely to risk a new adventure soon. A child who is made to endure an entire baseball season while loathing each game and practice will say, "No, thank you," to the next opportunity. Who will want to explore the possibility of playing the flute if they have to make a full-year commitment?

An alternative parenting stance that communicates the importance of keeping commitments while allowing the child some time and space to make an informed decision is needed. Develop parent talk that allows for a trial period and encourages follow-through once the commitment has been made.

> "Paul, if you want to sign up for the Saturday theater training, you'll need to check it out. If you want, you can go the first two weeks and see what it's like. After that you'll have to decide whether or not you want to make a summer commitment. Once they start rehearsals it would be unfair to the staff and other kids to back out."

> "So you want to sign up for band, eh? Sounds like fun. I'm willing to rent a trombone for six weeks while you check it out. Once we purchase one, though, you'll need to make a year-by-year commitment."

"Soccer is the first sport you've expressed interest in playing. Yes, I'm willing to support you with rides to practices and games. Once the season starts, there will be no turning back. You'll have to make up your mind about this after the third practice. Once you belong to a team, your teammates count on you to be there."

If a child quits something, that doesn't make him a quitter. It may just mean he's deep in the process of self-discovery. Perhaps your son learned gymnastics is not his thing. Maybe your daughter found that hockey looks like a lot more fun than it is. Or maybe she discovered she really didn't want to put the thousand-piece puzzle together after all.

Quitting may indeed be intelligent. How smart is it to endure something you dislike for six months just so you won't be called a quitter? Far better to attempt ten adventures, give up the eight you don't like, and concentrate on the other two, than to pick two, find out you hate them, and stick with them for their duration.

Listen to your parent talk surrounding the issue of quitting. Does your language encourage your children to attempt new things without the penalty of having to make a major commitment before they check it out? Or are you communicating that the risk of attempting new experiences is not worth the price they may have to pay?

Response-ability

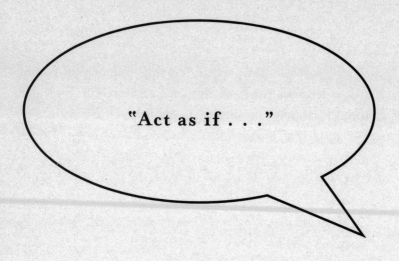

"Act as if . . ."

As parents, we hear "I can't" language all too often. It may occur as our child struggles with a long division assignment. It could take place as he attempts to master a new Nintendo game. Or it might be uttered as he works at reading directions for a recipe or instructions on how to build a model airplane. Whenever it occurs, "I can't" language signals an "I can't" attitude toward learning and achieving. Often accompanied by a whiny tone, "I can't" words are connected to "I can't" thinking, "I can't" believing, and "I can't" behaviors.

How do you respond when one of your children looks up from his study table and verbalizes some version of "I can't do it"? What do you say? If you're like many of the participants who attend my parent seminars, you reply with words similar to, "Sure you can, come on, try." Parents believe that if children would just try, they'd eventually prove to themselves that they can.

"Sure you can, come on, try" sounds like helpful parent talk. It is not because, most often, it doesn't work. Typically, children respond to our efforts to get them to try with "I'm trying" or "I tried already."

What children and parents don't realize is that *trying* doesn't work. Only *doing* works. Anyone busy *trying* is not busy *doing*. *Trying* is often an excuse for giving up.

A strategic piece of parent talk to replace the "Come on, try" language is *"Act as if. . . ."* The next time one of your children delivers a whiny rendition of "I can't," smile, look him in the eyes, speak from your heart, and give him these three words: *"Act as if."*

"Billy, *act as if* you can."
"Mary, I want you to *act as if* you already know how
to do this."
"Just *act as if* you've done this before, Shannon."

After you've delivered your new parent talk, step back, and go to another room. Watch from a distance as your child begins doing. I predict that you'll be pleasantly surprised by the effect of *"Act as if."* It won't work every time with every child, but it could be the most important phrase you add to your parent talk repertoire this year.

With young children, *"Pretend"* or *"Play like you can"* work well. *"Fake it"* and *"How would you do this if you did know?"* are effective alternatives with older children.

Sometimes you say *"Act as if"* and your child starts doing

the task incorrectly. Don't worry. You can correct incorrect doing, whereas it's impossible to correct someone who is not doing anything. *"Act as if"* gets children doing. You can adjust from there. Until they start doing, corrective guidance and feedback are impossible.

"Act as if" is more effective than "trying" because trying implies struggle, while "acting as if" is more playful and less serious. Some children won't *try* because if they don't succeed they consider themselves a failure. If they "pretend" or "act as if," no stigma or failure is attached.

Not sure *act as if* will work with your children? Not sure you can use it effectively? Why not *act as if* you can?

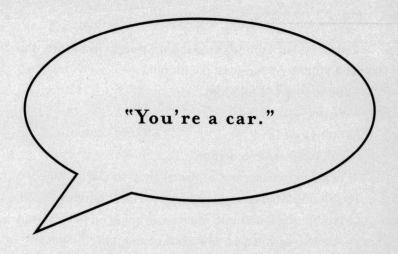

Matt, age six, came into the house crying hysterically. Tears flowed down his cheeks, and he couldn't catch his breath. I put him on my lap and held him close. His breathing slowed as I rubbed his back, but the stream of tears continued.

"What's wrong?" I asked as I continued to rub him.

"Randy," he blurted out between sobs.

"Randy hit you?"

"No."

"Randy knocked you down?"

"No."

"What?"

"Randy," sob, sob, "called me *stupid!*"

Randy was Matt's twelve-year-old brother, and occasionally he chose behaviors like calling Matt stupid.

"Randy called you stupid?" I repeated.

"Yes."

I turned Matt around, looked him straight in the eye, and launched into some unusual parent talk.

"You're a car!" I told him.

"What?"

"You're a car!"

"Dad, what are you doing?"

"I'm calling you a car. Car, Car, Car, Car, Car!"

By this time Matt had stopped crying. I had his full attention.

"Matt, there's something interesting going on here," I told him. "I'm calling you a car and you're not crying."

"Ya."

"Would you mind explaining that to me?"

"What do you mean?"

"I mean, I'm calling you a car and you're not crying. How come?"

"Dad," he offered with a disgusted look on his face, "I'm not a car!"

Then I had him. "Well, you know what, Matt? You're not stupid either."

"Oh," I heard him say, and I could see the wheels beginning to turn in his head.

Matt was having his first encounter with a concept that could positively affect the rest of his life. It is this:

MORE IMPORTANT THAN WHAT SOMEBODY
SAYS TO YOU IS WHAT YOU SAY TO YOURSELF
ABOUT WHAT THEY SAY TO YOU.

When my parent talk was, "You're a car," Matt said to himself, "No, I'm not," or "What is my dad doing?" or "He sure doesn't know me." When Randy called him stupid, he could have said to himself, "No, I'm not," or "What's the matter with Randy?" or "He sure doesn't know me."

You can't control the entire world and get everyone to talk to you just the way you want to be talked to. But you can *always* control how you talk to yourself about how others talk to you. Making *your* talk more important than *their* talk is a sign of maturity and self-responsibility and a skill we can help our children learn.

Teach your children where their power truly is. Help them appreciate the fact that their power is not in controlling what others say to them. Their power lies within and is regulated by how they choose to talk to themselves.

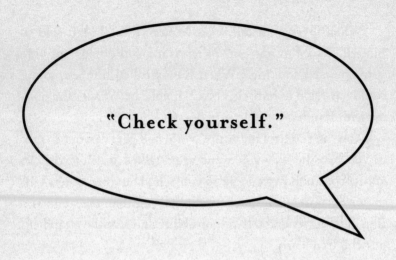

"Check yourself."

"Check yourself" is a quick phrase that is useful and adaptable with any age child. It can be used with young children as a reminder about noise. "I'm having difficulty concentrating. *Please check yourself* to hear if you're using your twelve-inch voice." It can be used with middle-school-age children to help them prepare for study time. "It's almost seven. *Check yourself* to see if you have all the needed materials." When you're getting ready to go for a long drive, you can gently remind children, *"Check yourself* to see that you have all the items in your car kit you'll need for the trip."

"Check yourself" can be used with older children as a way to help them learn what is expected on specific issues.

"At camp you'll need these four things. *Check yourself* to see if you have them adequately covered."

"Sweeping off the sidewalk and making sure the gas can has been put away are two things that are important when mowing the grass. *Check yourself* to see if you have these handled."

When you add *"Check yourself"* to your parent talk and use it frequently in your language patterns, you send a positive message to your children. You're telling them by your language and your actions that it is *their* job to check on themselves, not yours. You step out of the authoritarian, rescuing role and give them the opportunity to choose self-responsibility in their lives.

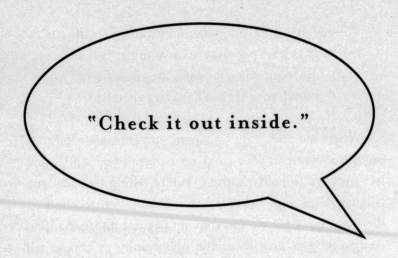

"Check it out inside."

Both teachers and parents teach children where to turn for answers. We show them how to look up answers in the dictionary, consult experts, examine an encyclopedia, read the newspaper, or we equip them with the skills necessary to use a reference librarian effectively. We teach them to look to a variety of resources for answers, but rarely do we teach them to look inside themselves.

"Check it out inside" is a phrase that helps us to help children look within for answers. Each of us has a wise part within, an intuitive part that knows what is best for us. Learning how to contact, listen to, and trust that inner authority are important skills. They are invaluable when life presents us with problems whose answers are not found in the back of the book.

"Not sure which part to audition for the play?
Check it out inside."

"Should you join your friends for a smoke after
school? *Check in.*"
"Unclear how to proceed with your term paper? *Listen
to the voice within.*"
"Wondering who to vote for in the class election? *Check
it out inside.*"

It is crucial that we help our children develop a healthy
sense of competence. This includes a feeling of confidence in
their own knowledge and ability to make decisions. Children
who don't feel competent often experience feelings of helplessness and insecurity about their ability to make minor decisions and major life choices. Such people learn to rely on
others and may search everywhere for answers and for happiness except inside themselves. They fail to develop individual
standards or a strong internal sense of self. Parents can contribute to a child's sense of security and self-confidence by
encouraging autonomy and competence with phrases like
"Check it out inside."

"Check it out inside" is a piece of parent talk that teaches
the child to trust his *own* judgment. It helps him develop as an
independent, autonomous individual capable of making personal decisions. Having faith in his own inner authority serves
a child well by enabling him to resist the temptation to please
others at his own expense or to compromise himself by con-
forming to peer pressure. The child who has learned to *"check
it out inside"* has been given "life assurance." He can trust his
own judgment regarding drugs, sex, and alcohol instead of
relying on the judgment of his peer group.

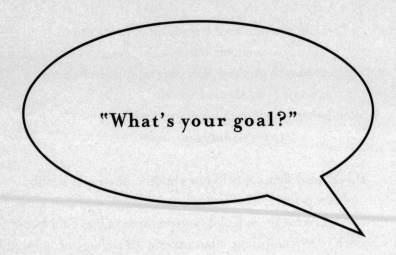

"What's your goal?"

Many children live their lives like cows. A cow wakes up in the morning, walks out of the barn, looks down, sees a clump of grass, bends down, and eats it. Then it sees another clump of grass and eats that one, too. Then another. This process continues until about noon, when the cow looks up, sees the barn a hundred yards away, and says to herself, "Oh, I'm over here." The cow has no idea of how she got there or where she's going. Her only concern is that next clump of grass in front of her.

For too many children that next clump of grass is the focal point in their lives. They have no clear vision of where they are going or what they want to accomplish. Without a specific direction, it's difficult for them to chart a course. If they don't know where they're going, they won't even know when they get there. That's where *"What's your goal?"* comes in.

"What's your goal?" is parent talk that helps the child to focus. It gets him thinking about direction, about the intended outcome, about his desired destination. Other versions of *"What's your goal?"* include:

"What are you trying to accomplish?"
"Where do you want to get to?"
"What would you be happy with?"
"What are you shooting for?"
"What do you really want to achieve?"
"What is it that you want out of this?"

With a clear goal in mind, it's easier for children to create a plan to achieve it. Once the goal is defined and understood, ideas about possible activities for accomplishing that goal can flow. Use parent talk to help your children appreciate the connection between their actions and achieving a goal. Ask them, *"What can you do to move closer to your goal?"* or *"What are some things you can do to get there?"* *"What activities will help you attain the goal?"* works well, also.

Help children make their goals specific. "I want to do better in math" is a general goal that is difficult to measure accurately. How can the child tell when he gets there? Where is that point at which he can pat himself on the back and say, "Yes, I did it!"

A more specific goal is "I want to get ninety percent or better on my math test this week." Now his goal is measurable, and the child can tell whether or not he accomplished it.

"What's your goal?" is parent talk that helps your children think in terms of outcomes. It helps them to create vision, mis-

sion, and purpose in their lives. It helps them see themselves as part of a goal-oriented family that does much more than wander aimlessly through life accepting whichever clump of grass comes their way next.

Goal setting is empowering. It most often leads to goal achievement. This practice helps children obtain tangible evidence to support a view of themselves as achievers. When children perceive themselves as achievers, they act more like achievers. When they act more like achievers, they achieve more. This process becomes a delicious cycle that every parent would love to encourage. Isn't that one of your goals?

"SKIPPING MIDDLE SCHOOL ISN'T REALLY THE KIND OF GOAL WE HAD IN MIND."

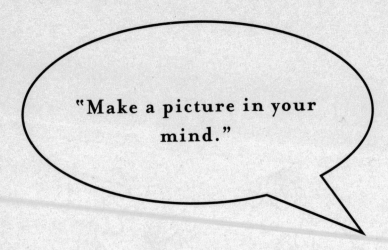

"Make a picture in your mind."

Quiet yourself for a moment. Relax and breathe deeply. Make a picture in your mind of yourself using helpful, new language patterns with your family. See yourself having fun with the examples presented in this book. Notice your enthusiasm as you play with this style of language. Watch as your children react positively. See them responding in ways that indicate increased self-responsibility and feelings of self-worth. Notice how they cooperate with one another and behave interdependently. Watch as their behaviors indicate an increasing sense of personal power and self-esteem.

Now picture yourself at the end of the evening. See yourself relaxed, satisfied, fulfilled. Notice how pleased you are with yourself, your emerging language patterns, and the results you are getting. Enjoy the pictures for a few moments. Then, read on.

The activity above is called *positive picturing* or *mental rehearsal.* It involves the use of the imagination to picture the positive process and outcome of an upcoming activity. Using the technique as it is described above will help you achieve your new language goals.

One element significantly related to achievement is the ability to visualize desired outcomes. Chances are, if you are not able to imagine yourself behaving in a certain way, you will not be able to behave that way. If you cannot see yourself using this style of language, you may not use it. By creating a positive picture in your mind, you increase the odds for success.

Positive picturing is a strategy you can use with children of any age. Young children can make a picture in their minds of finding just the right book on their excursion to the library. Before your teen goes for a job interview, help him to visualize it in his mind.

"Make a picture in your mind" is parent talk that helps clarify your expectations to your children. Use this language to specify the behaviors and levels of performance you desire.

As you tuck your ten-year-old into bed, have him picture himself getting ready for school in the morning. Ask him to visualize getting up on time, packing a lunch, getting his backpack, and arriving at the bus stop before the bus arrives.

Teachers also use this technique to help their students. I know one teacher who uses this strategy prior to every assembly.

"Children," she begins, "close your eyes gently and relax. Make a picture in your mind of our class walking quietly into the gym, single file, arms at our sides. Notice one of your friends calling out to you. You smile and nod your head silently. Look! Every member of the class has taken their seat quickly and watches the front. Feel your pride and sense of maturity as you are quietly unaffected by those around you."

Another teacher I observed used mental rehearsal to introduce an activity. It allowed students to experience the situation mentally before they attempted it physically.

"Today we will be painting at the easel for the first time. Close your eyes and see yourself approach the easel. Stop now and push up your sleeves. Take a paint shirt from the hook and put it on backwards. See? The buttons are on the back. Ask a friend to fasten the top button for you. Who did you ask? See them in your mind. Now you are ready to paint. Choose a color, pick up a brush, and gently wipe it on the side of the cup. See? Now there are very few drips while you paint. Watch yourself place the brush back into the color that matches. That way the colors won't get mixed in the cups. Notice how you remember to mix the colors on your paper. Stroke, dab, swirl. Enjoy creating your picture.

"Okay, now your painting is done. Oh, you like it so much that you decide to leave it right on the easel to dry so it won't get messed up. See yourself take the sponge out of the bucket and squeeze the water out. You wipe up all the paint drips off the floor without leaving any puddles! Now you wash your hands and dry them. Remove the paint shirt and replace it on the hook. Stand back and admire your artwork. Feel how responsible and capable you are!"

Does visualizing the process of using the easel insure that colors will not get mixed? Does it eliminate drips on paintings, messes on floors, and confusion at the easel? Of course not. It will, however, increase your chances of getting what you want more of the time.

Positive picturing will help you influence how your children see themselves and, consequently, how they perform. Children who see themselves as leaders act like leaders. Children who see themselves as readers act like readers.

Positive picturing will help your children reach their goals. Children can visualize themselves making the basketball team, writing in cursive, or reading fluently. They can see themselves driving the car, building a sandcastle, or getting the job. The ability to visualize a desire is one big step towards attaining it. Repetitive positive picturing empowers children by teaching them that they can direct their own thoughts and imagination toward achieving a desired result.

When you ask your youngster to make a picture in his mind, you engage his right brain. That is the part of the brain that thinks holistically and is responsible for imagination and intuition. Since most school instruction involves the logical, linear, left brain, positive picturing helps create a balance. When the child involves the whole brain, learning increases and success multiplies.

Once again, quiet yourself for a moment. Relax and breathe deeply. Make a picture in your mind of yourself using positive picturing with your children. Rehearse mentally, seeing yourself as successful. Feel the feelings associated with success. Enjoy your excitement as well as theirs. Review the entire scene in your mind as you experience satisfaction. Know that this mental rehearsal is moving you closer to using this strategy effectively with your family. Expect that you will be skilled in telling your children, *"Make a picture in your mind."*

"Soon I'll be gone."

"Soon I'll be gone" is parent talk that begins as a speech and eventually evolves into a one-liner. It is appropriate for any child who resists or complains about parental monitoring.

Monitoring is an important function of parenting. At times we have to monitor homework, chores, and other childhood responsibilities. Children, especially teenagers, don't always appreciate or understand the necessity of our performing that role. They complain, "Why do you always have to check up on me?" or ask, "Don't you trust me to do this myself?" That's when a good *"Soon I'll be gone"* speech becomes an important piece of your parent talk skills.

Tanya, thirteen, complained to her father that she didn't like him checking up on her after she cleaned her room. His response was a classic *"Soon I'll be gone"* speech. He told her, *"Tanya, you've got just a few more years here with your mother and me until you get out on your own. My responsibility as your father during that time is to teach you all the things that are necessary for you to live effectively on your own. One of the things I need to teach you during those few years I have left before you're grown and on your own is how to be neat, clean, and organized. If I check your room and find it meets the standard three times in a row, I'll figure you've got this one under control and I'll be gone. Until that occurs, I'll assume you still need my help."*

What Tanya's father actually communicated to his teenager without saying these exact words was, "If you can show me you can do it by yourself, I'm out of here. You want me to be history? Then prove you can handle it. Soon I'll be gone, and it's up to you just how soon."

Jesse, a fifth grader, took exception with his mother's consistent review of his efforts to cut the grass. She responded to his complaint with her version of *"Soon I'll be gone."* "Sounds like you don't like me checking on you. We're in agreement on that one because I don't like checking on you either. I'll be glad when I don't have to do it anymore. As soon as you can show me that I've accomplished my task of teaching you how to mow the grass effectively, I'll be gone. Show me three times in a row that you can remember the four basics of cutting and the two critical cleanup procedures and you're on your own. Until then, you're stuck with me."

After delivering several repetitions of your *"Soon I'll be gone"* speech, you can shorten it to one sentence.

"When you show me you can handle it, *I'm history.*"
"Want me gone?" Prove by your behavior that you've got it."

"The quickest way to get to do this by yourself is to show me
you can do it without supervision."
"Soon I'll be gone. Just show me you don't need me."

Monitoring is a task that is not enjoyed by either the monitor or the one being monitored. To fulfill your responsibility
as the one who monitors the skills you taught and to step out
of that role as quickly as the child's acceptance of responsibility allows, add *"Soon I'll be gone"* language to your parent talk.

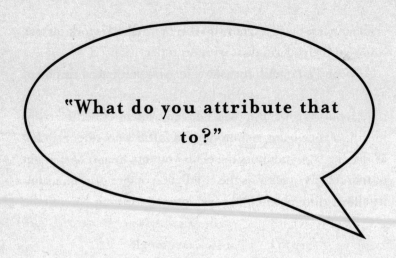

"What do you attribute that to?"

Increase your children's sense of personal power and get attribute theory working in their lives with parent talk phrases that help them see the connection between their efforts (cause) and the results that follow (effect).

"You got an A in science? *What do you attribute that to?*"
"You got the job? Wonderful. *How did you pull that off?*"
"You tie your own shoes without any help now. *How did that happen?*"
"So your dad says you're grounded. *How did you produce that result?*"

Children with strong self-esteem feel empowered and in control in their lives. They attribute the effects they create to something they have control over. They see their effort, energy, persistence, determination, and hard work as the causes of their success.

In contrast, children with low self-esteem feel impotent and out of control in their lives. They attribute the effects they create to some force outside of themselves. They attribute their success or lack of success to luck, magic, circumstance, who they know, or being in the right place at the right time.

Read through the following conversation and see if you can identify where the mother used parent talk filled with attribute theory to help her son see himself as cause.

"Mom, I got an A on my report card. I aced driver's training!"

"Let me see. Sure enough. Congratulations, Son. What do you attribute that to?"

"What do you mean?"

"How did you do that? That's the first A you've had in high school. How did you get it?"

"The teacher gave it to me. He's really good, fun to listen to, interesting."

"So the teacher is responsible for your A?"

"Yes."

"You had that teacher last semester for literature. You didn't get an A in that class."

"That's different. This class was important. I wanted to get an A to show you I knew this stuff so you'd let me use the car."

"So you decided to do well in this class!"

"Yes."

"So what did you do?"

"What do you mean?"

"Once you decided to do well, how did you go about it? How did you create that A?"

"One thing I did was leave my friends in the back of the room and sit down close to the teacher. In my other classes I sit with my friends and we talk a lot."

"Anything else?"

"I listened to everything the teacher said and wrote down what I thought was important."

"So you took notes?"

"Yes."

"Anything else?"

"I read all the chapters, some of them twice."

"Is there more?"

"I studied for the tests."

"Let me see if I've got this right. When you decide to do well in a class, you sit by the teacher, take notes, read the material, and study for the tests?"

"That's it."

"Okay. I wondered how you did that. Thanks for sharing. And congratulations again on the A."

"Thanks, Mom."

In the scenario above the parent continued to structure her parent talk in a way that helped the child focus on his own efforts, actions, choices, and attitudes. She used attribute theory to focus her son on the role he played in creating this result (an A in driver's training) in his life.

Attribute theory can be used to help children own both the positive and the negative effects in their lives.

"So you made the team. What do you attribute that to?"

or

"So you got cut from the team. What do you attribute that to?"

"You were in time-out twice today? What do you do to get in time-out?"

or

"No time-outs today. What do you do to stay out of time-out?"

Using language that helps children see themselves as an active force in their lives empowers them. It helps them step out of the victim stance and take charge of their lives.

As you make attribute theory a regular part of your parent talk, watch and enjoy as your children take increased ownership for the results they create.

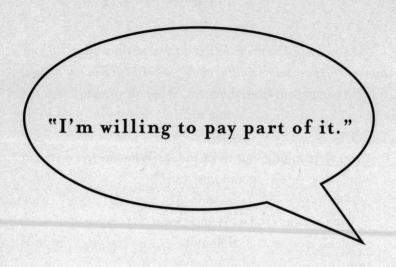

"I'm willing to pay part of it."

"Mom, can I have that pair of jeans, please?"
"I'd look great in those sneakers. I've just got to have them."
"Would you buy this game for me, Dad?"

As parents, we're continually bombarded with questions like these. Our children want things. They want a new bike, jacket, tennis shoes, computer, car, or Beanie Baby. We then assume the role of doing the thinking, making a decision, and informing the child. Most of the time our response is either "yes" or "no."

An alternative to getting trapped in the "yes or no" role of permission giver is to use parent talk that forces the child to do the thinking. Try communicating your willingness to pay a portion of the price and see if the child is willing to pay the difference.

"I have sixty dollars in my budget for sneakers. These cost one hundred dollars. I'd be willing to pay what I have in my budget. You'll have to come up with the rest." Now the child is required to enter the thinking mode. He has to decide just how badly he wants the sneakers and determine how that fits with his other priorities. Sometimes children decide they don't want the object that much and decline your offer. Other times they're firm in their desire and contribute funds to get what they want. Either way, offering to pay a portion of the full price helps you and the child determine his true level of desire.

In addition to forcing children to think, offering to pay only a portion of the price has other advantages. Feelings of ownership increase when children invest some of their own money to obtain what they want. They're more likely to take better care of a bicycle they helped purchase than one that was given to them. Respect for clothing is greater when the child has used some of his own money to obtain it.

Feelings of personal power expand when children see themselves as capable of satisfying some of their own wants. Parents who buy all their children's belongings rob them of opportunities to feel capable and responsible. These young-sters miss a chance to see their power in action and to wear or use visible proof of their capableness. Your willingness to let them pay also carries with it your willingness to allow their access to feelings of power and increasing responsibility.

To empower your children, nudge them into a thinking mode, help them determine what they really desire, and use parent talk that communicates your position of not buying top-of-the-line products. Tell your child, *"I'll pay two thirds of it,"* or *"My budget can handle only part of the price. I'll pay half if you'll pay the rest."* Then stand back and observe how their struggle with the dilemma moves them to a place of greater self-responsibility.

"YOU THINK YOU'VE GOT IT TOUGH! MY PARENTS HAVE BEEN GOING TO PARENTING SEMINARS!"

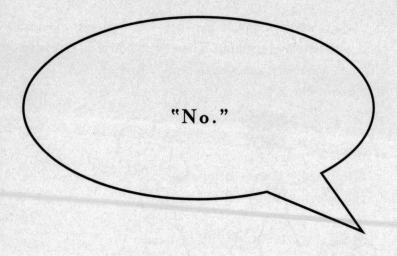

"No."

If you're not telling your children *"no"* on occasion, you are doing them a disservice. Children need to hear the word *no*. Youngsters deserve to know there are adults in their lives who will draw lines and enforce them, consistently and lovingly.

Of course, children push and test the limits. They want to know where the line is. Our job is to draw it. Theirs is to protest and resist. Children will do their job. It's up to us as parents to do ours.

When children push and test the limits, we often interpret their actions to mean "I want the limits changed." More often the limit testing really means "Please show me there is someone in my life who will not cave in and surrender every time I create a test. Please be the adult, so I can relax with being a child."

"No" can be a complete sentence. Often parents overexplain with lengthy reasoning. There is no power in excessive verbiage. Authority comes from brevity. Just say, *"No."*

Yes, you can give a reason for the *no*. I suggest you keep the explanation simple and allow no arguing. Reasons are given so children will know the reason, not so they can have an invitation to argue, whine, or pout.

Occasionally parents make *no* sound like they are asking the child's permission to say it. For example:

"Can I go to the mall today?"
"No, because you came back late yesterday and didn't
call, okay?"

You don't need your child's permission to tell him "no." You're the parent. You get to say "no."

With preadolescents and teenagers it can be easier to say "yes" than "no." Since this age group is often into proving their power and resisting, they don't take "no" well.

If you respond to your teen's request to spend the night at Becky's with: "No, not until you clean your bedroom and finish your chore in the garage," she's not likely to hear the words *garage* or *bedroom*. As soon as the word *no* registers, she'll get her back up, shut down the listening apparatus, and begin stacking up arguments in her head. She may even interrupt your parent talk before you get to the words *garage* and *bedroom*. Emotion and power plays get activated. Listening goes into hibernation.

For better results to the overnight inquiry, add "yes" to your parent talk. The dialogue now sounds like this:

"Can I spend the night at Becky's?"
"Yes! As soon as you clean your room and finish your
chore in the garage."

Only one word has been changed in this dialogue. By
replacing *no* with *yes,* you'll get a more favorable response, less
resistance, and less resentment. As soon as your child hears
"yes," she'll relax and be more likely to hear the rest of your
parent talk. Hearing your whole message, she may conclude
that the overnight at Becky's is within her reach. She'll likely
see herself as being in control and may begin immediately to
take steps to get what she wants.

When you do say "no," I suggest you don't change your
mind. If you say "no" and your child argues with you and
keeps up the pressure until you change your response, you've
just taught her that your "no" means "You haven't made my
life miserable enough yet for me to change my mind. If you
keep after me for a while longer, I'll probably change my
answer."

To teach a child that "no" means *no,* let your "no" *mean* no.

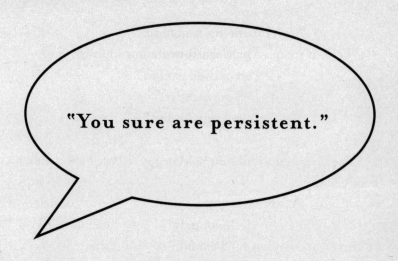

"You sure are persistent."

It was once believed that an individual's IQ was relatively fixed. From the time it could be measured there was little we could do to raise it, no matter how much stimulation or education we provided. Now we know that one's IQ is variable and that, through mental and emotional nourishment and education, there can be significant improvements. We also know that even with an increase in a child's IQ, there will be little change in her ability to succeed and be happy if her self-concept remains negative. Self-esteem, it seems, is as important to quality of life as intelligence is. In other words, a child's "I am's" are as important as her IQ.

"I am's" are the core beliefs that children hold about themselves. Many children have core beliefs that are positive.

"I am capable."
"I am athletic."

"I am mathematical."
"I am worthwhile."
"I am a child of God."
"I am creative."
"I am responsible."

Likewise, many children hold negative core beliefs about themselves.

"I am ugly."
"I am fat."
"I am uncoordinated."
"I am not wanted."
"I am stupid."
"I am not good enough."
"I am wrong."

"I am's" are formed early in life. Kindergarten teachers will tell you that their five-year-old students come to school with "I am's" already in place. These youngsters enter the formal educational process already holding firm beliefs about themselves. Some of these beliefs serve them well: "I am attractive," "I can learn what I want to learn," "I am musical." Others are erroneous or limiting: "I am dumb," "I am a troublemaker," "I am a klutz." Whether positive or negative, the self-beliefs that students hold at the beginning of kindergarten influence them throughout their entire lives. That is why I call them Life Sentences.

Life Sentences are critical because behavior flows from beliefs. If a child believes he's uncoordinated, he acts uncoordinated. Since that belief is firmly rooted in his consciousness, he's more likely to slip, trip, or stumble than someone who believes he's athletic. The youngster who believes he's uncoordinated is also more likely to interpret events in ways that are consistent with that belief. The child's internal dialogue following a spilled glass of milk may be, "There I go again, an uncoordinated klutz. That's the way *I am*." Over time he will prove to himself, "I am uncoordinated."

Imagine two children approaching the task of riding a two-wheeled bike for the first time. One has the positive Life Sentence: "I am athletic." The other has a negative Life Sentence: "I am a klutz." The child with the negative Life Sentence approaches the bike tentatively. His eyes are cast downward. His step is slow and unsure. He touches the bike tentatively, suspiciously. His body language and behaviors all indicate "I can't." The child with the positive Life Sentence approaches the bike with confidence. There is power in his stride and strength in his grip of the handlebars. He is eager to begin. He acts as if he can.

Who do you believe will learn to ride the bike first? Which Life Sentence will be most helpful in learning this new skill?

Life Sentences are formed early in life and may remain relatively fixed throughout. Still, parents have great influence because during childhood and adolescence Life Sentences are not yet firmly set in the consciousness. A skillful parent can grant reprieves and commute Life Sentences by how she talks to her children.

Parents are like mirrors, constantly reflecting back to their children what we think of them. They look at those reflections and say to themselves, "Oh, so that is what *I am*." We can strengthen or weaken a Life Sentence by the attitudes we reflect.

David Elkind, an early childhood expert, tells a story about the day he accepted a negative Life Sentence during vocal music class. The teacher was preparing the children for a musical production. During practice she leveled a finger straight at young David and announced, "Elkind, you're a mouther." A mouther was a person who didn't get to sing but could only move his mouth and pretend. Since that time, David Elkind has held the belief that "I am not a singer." Thankfully, another one of young Elkind's teachers told him, "You have a flair for writing." That comment was certainly one important contribution to what became a Life Sentence of "I am a writer."

Recently, I overheard a parent tell his child, *"You sure are persistent."*

"What is 'persistent'?" asked the youngster.

"Persistent is what you were while you were learning your multiplication tables. You worked on your sixes over the weekend. You practiced them Monday night, Tuesday night, and Wednesday night. On Thursday you passed the skills test. You kept at it until you got it. That's persistent."

"Yes," said the ten-year-old as he walked away. "I sure am persistent."

Parents make minute-to-minute choices throughout every day about what behaviors to notice, what to mention, what to put under the magnifying glass. In every home there is evidence of cooperation and lack of cooperation. There are acts of responsibility and acts of irresponsibility. It's possible to perceive helpfulness or unhelpfulness, initiative or procrastination. We decide what to see. We choose what we will mention and what we'll reflect back to children through our parent talk. These choices must be carefully made so that we have a positive influence on our children's Life Sentences.

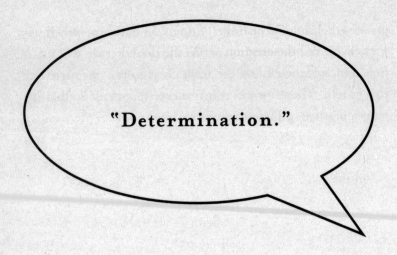

"Determination."

Ranae's mother waited and watched while her five-year-old worked for more than ten minutes putting her socks on. With the task complete, this parent gave her daughter a big bonding smile and uttered one word: *"Determination."*

Gerardo's father assisted with his son's effort to master multiplication tables by using flash cards to give the boy practice. Following one week's worth of practice sessions, Gerardo presented his parents with a school paper that revealed one hundred percent correct on a multiplication work sheet. His father's comment was short and to the point. *"Persistence,"* he said, as he placed his hand on Gerardo's shoulder and gave a light squeeze.

Pamela's grandfather observed in stunned silence as she constructed a vehicle from the pieces of the erector set he had given her on her birthday. *"Ingenuity,"* he responded, as Pamela moved the creation across the floor.

In each of these cases, the adult chose to use a highly effective parent talk strategy: *Sum it up in one word.* To use this strategy, observe your child and determine which positive attribute she is displaying. Pick one word that summarizes that attribute and say it aloud with no other words attached. All of these work well:

"Caring."
"Self-control."
"Faith."
"Willpower."
"Effort."
"Follow-through."
"Love."
"Courage."
"Appreciation."
"Honesty."
"Responsibility."
"Respect."

Add a smile, a wink, or a pat on the back to your verbalization to increase its effectiveness.

It is important that the one word you use be a summary of the attribute rather than an evaluation of the child or her creation. "Good," "beautiful," "excellent," "tremendous," "fantastic," "super," "stupendous," and "awesome" are examples of evaluations and need to be avoided.

By using one word to communicate your reaction, you increase the odds that the message will register with your child. With no other words to detract from it, *"determination"* will have a powerful effect. So will *persistence, effort, caring,* or any other positive attribute you notice and communicate with one word.

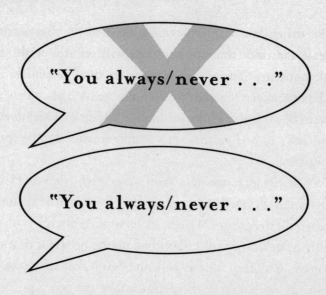

Pay attention to the words *always* and *never*. Used indiscriminately, they can communicate negative expectations to your children.

"Why do you *always* interrupt me?"
"You *always* blame someone else."
"You *never* attempt to do anything extra."

When parents use *always* and *never* to direct accusing statements at their children, they brand the children as being *that way*. Children who see themselves a certain way are more likely to act *that way*. Therefore, the parent talk that accompanies *always* and *never* actually reinforces the behavior you want to eliminate.

A problem for parents who use *always* and *never* is that it diverts the child's attention away from the issue that needs to be dealt with and focuses it on the accusation. A typical internal response to "You always have to be first" is denial. The child remembers the one time, three years ago, when she chose to be last. She is now so busy thinking that she doesn't *always* have to be first that she's unable to attend to the present situation.

When parents remark, "You *never* give up," or "I can *always* count on you," children may be pleased with the praise, yet discredit the praiser. They may focus their attention on the validity of the statement rather than on the behavior that was endorsed. Children know at some level that *always/never* statements are not true. Sometimes they do give up. Occasionally they're not dependable. If they determine that the statement is a fallacy, they may discredit the speaker as well as the statement. Their self-talk might be:

> "My mom's pretty dumb."
> "Don't believe anything Dad says."
> "She doesn't know me very well."
> "Somehow I fooled him into thinking I'm something
> I'm not."

When you wish to communicate positive expectancy by praising in this manner, I suggest you change your parent talk to include the words *usually* and *most of the time*.

> "I can usually depend on you to finish your chores without
> being reminded."
> "Most of the time, I can count on you to be right on time."

Now your parent talk is consistent with reality and helps children focus on and internalize the positive message you want to send.

Sometimes children imitate our use of *always* and *never*.

"She *always* strikes out."
"He *never* passes the ball to me."
"He *never* stops talking about himself."
"She *always* gives homework."

Children use these words when they are complaining or disowning.

"You *never* give me a chance."
"You *always* let him sit in front."

You can help children hear that their statements are all-inclusive generalizations by asking *"What do you mean, 'always'?"* or *"What do you mean, 'never'?"* These gentle questions will help them refocus on what they really mean.

"I want a turn, Mom."
"Can I sit in front this time?"

Free your parent talk from sweeping generalizations when giving children feedback. Save *always* and *never* for those rare instances when they are accurate descriptors.

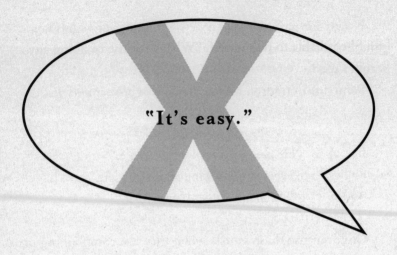

"It's easy."

Barbara sat hunched over, tightly gripping her pencil. Signs of exasperation revealed her frustration with long division. Barbara's father observed her efforts closely, then decided to intervene. Wanting to encourage the child and communicate his faith in her abilities and intelligence, he explained the process of long division. Then he whispered, "Come on, Barbara, you can do it. It's easy." He did not know that these simple words of encouragement had trapped Barbara in a no-win situation.

The parent who encourages with *"It's easy"* may initiate feelings of fear in the child. Barbara is afraid of appearing incompetent. "He says it's easy," she says to herself. "What if I can't do it? My friends will think I'm stupid."

By putting faith in her father's words, "It's easy," Barbara may lose faith in herself. If she attempts the task because she trusts her dad and wants to please him, she risks failure. Failing at something "easy," she may feel discouraged and hopeless. She is liable to tell herself, "What's the use of doing anything? I can't even do something easy. I must be stupid."

On the other hand, Barbara may use the adult's parent talk to get herself started. She may breeze through the long division and discover that it *was* easy for her. What amount of satisfaction can she feel for completing a task that was already pronounced *easy?* She'll probably feel only relief that she was able to do it without appearing foolish. "Of course I did it," goes her internal dialogue. "Anybody can do it. After all, it's easy."

A different possibility is that Barbara may complete the task successfully but with great difficulty. Instead of feeling proud, she may believe that a difficult task would be beyond her ability because she had to struggle to complete something *easy.* Since "easy" tasks are hard for her, she may question her own intelligence. Her self-talk may be, "Even if I work my hardest, I can only do something easy. I must be stupid."

In each of these situations, Barbara can only lose by attempting a task that the parent has pronounced "easy."

When you want children to *win,* and you wish to communicate your faith in them, I suggest that you change the parent talk "It's easy" to *"I think you're ready for this."*

"I think you're ready for this" does not address the difficulty of the task. That interpretation is left to the child. The phrase communicates the parent's opinion of the child's skill level *at that time,* regardless of the degree of difficulty the child attaches to the task. If the child succeeds, she can say to herself, "I was ready for this. I did it!" She can enjoy the accomplishment and experience satisfaction according to her own

assessment of how hard she worked. If she doesn't succeed, she can say, "I guess I'm not ready for this *yet*," comforted by the parent's confidence and her own assurance that she will be successful in the future when she *is* ready.

Your choice of language helps children create self-talk that affirms their capabilities and strengthens their self-esteem. You can communicate faith in their competence and encourage their efforts. Eliminate *"It's easy"* from your parent talk. I think you're ready for this.

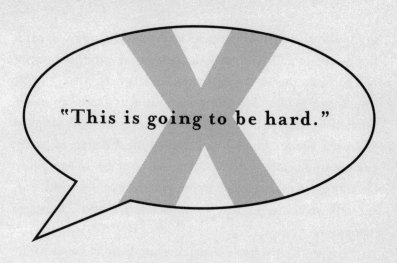

"This is going to be hard."

"This team is going to be difficult to beat."
"That acrobatic routine is tough."
"Second grade is a lot harder than first grade!"

These sentences are all variations of the same theme. Each is an attempt to impress on children the seriousness of an upcoming activity. Each is delivered as a gentle warning. Each may be more harmful than helpful.

Warnings, though well intentioned, plant doubt in children's minds. They are negative predictors of things to come and are often the first step in a string of events that lead to a self-fulfilling prophesy.

If your parent talk frequently reminds your first grader of the difficulties that await her the following year, she will develop negative expectations and come to believe that second grade is difficult. Her perception of second grade will cause her to create a "hard" second-grade experience because she will focus on the aspects that match her beliefs.

Warnings like "That acrobatic routine is tough" are sometimes delivered so that children will take the task seriously and work harder. One unspoken message this style of parent talk communicates is that we believe the child isn't responsible enough to take the task seriously unless we scare her. Parent talk that creates fear is never an effective long-term motivator.

I suggest that you avoid negative predictions. Concentrate instead on giving children the information necessary to make their own determinations about levels of difficulty. Replace words like *hard, difficult,* or *tough* with clear descriptions. Simply give them the facts. "There are two new steps in this routine, and it requires three neck springs in the sequence."

Instead of warning children about second grade, tell them specifically what is expected in that grade. Detail some of the skills and learning that will be covered without mentioning difficulty.

When you concentrate on giving children information without projecting negative expectations, your words help move them toward your goal of having them take the acrobatic routine, the team, or second grade seriously.

"That's impossible."

Five-year-old Shasta told her mother she wanted to go to Disney World for her birthday. William, age ten, let it be known that he wanted to be an astronaut when he grew up. Brenda, a high school junior, began talking about her desire to attend an out-of-state college. In each case a parent reacted with *"That's impossible."*

"That's not realistic," "That can't happen," "There's no way," "You can forget that one," and "That's impossible" are parent talk phrases that shrink our children and make them little in their own eyes. This type of response is parent-inflicted bondage that ties our children in place and keeps them stuck. It shuts off possibility in their lives and places limits on their dreams.

Children need support and encouragement for their dreams. They need parents who don't know, use, or believe the words "That's impossible" and "It's no use." They deserve parents who talk in ways that give them a sense of their unlimitedness and help them to see possibility in their lives.

Replace "There's no way" with *"You can do anything you want, if you want it bad enough."* Change "You can forget that one" to *"When you set your mind to something, you're usually able to find a way."* Drop "That can't happen" from your parent talk and add *"Where there's a will, there's a way."*

"But that isn't being realistic," a mother argued at one of my seminars. "My son can't be a professional athlete with his body, and the sooner he realizes it, the better off he'll be."

"Maybe he will and maybe he won't become a professional athlete," I told her. "At this point no one knows for sure. What we do know for sure is that your words will become his boundaries. Your words will confine and limit him. Your words will choke off any possibility of him achieving his dream or of even keeping it alive for awhile. *Realistic* is in the mind of the beholder. What's *unrealistic* to one person is a challenge to be overcome to another. There are numerous cases of people achieving far beyond the 'realistic' judgments of parents and coaches."

"But I can't tell my son I think he'll become a pro football player when I know he won't," the mother persisted.

Don't miss the point here. I'm not suggesting you tell your child that he will achieve his dream. You don't know that he will. You don't know that he won't, either. So why play on either side of that equation? Instead, aim your parent talk at your child's determination, persistence, or ingenuity.

I'm not advocating that you tell your child she can go to an out-of-state college, only that you don't rip her dream away before she has an opportunity to explore the realities of it herself. *"Where there's a will, there's a way"* leaves the dream intact and sends the child an affirmative message about how you perceive her determination. *"When you decide you want something, you usually find a way to get it"* says nothing about going or not going to Disney World. It talks about the child's ingenuity. *"You can do anything you want to if you want it badly enough"* takes no position on whether or not you think the child can become an astronaut. It speaks to persistence and encourages lofty goals and high aspirations.

Your words become your children's boundaries. Your language limits their vision and the awareness of possibilities that exist for them. Your choice of words helps sculpt their beliefs about who they are and what they can become. Drop limits and add possibility to your children's lives by removing the language of limitation from your parent talk.

The Search for
Solutions

"Sounds like you have a problem."

Justin concentrated deeply on the schoolwork before him. As he bore down on his work and his pencil, the lead snapped. Without hesitation, he approached the teacher and announced, "My pencil broke." The next move was up to Mr. Richardson, Justin's teacher. He could choose from a variety of responses:

"Borrow one from a friend."
"Here, use one of these."
"You can sharpen it now, if you wish."
"You'll have to wait until later."

Each of these possible responses represents a teacher taking responsibility for a student's problem. Each communicates, "I'll take over. I'll solve the problem." Each indicates a lack of respect for the child's ability and willingness to manage a piece of his own school life.

"Sounds like you have a problem," Mr. Richardson told Justin. With those words he kept the responsibility for the solution to the problem with Justin, where it belonged. He reminded Justin just who owned the problem and sent a silent message that he trusted Justin to come up with a reasonable solution. Justin did that. "I guess I'll have to borrow one," he replied, and returned to his seat.

Sometimes, *"Sounds like you have a problem"* is enough to prompt children into the search for and discovery of a solution. When it is not, follow your message with, *"I know you can handle it."* Again, this tells children that you see them as problem solvers and that you have confidence in their abilities in this area.

"Sounds like you have a problem" is also useful parent talk when kids tattle.

"Bobby called me a name."
"Marcy won't let me have a turn."
"Terry took my pencil."

In each case, *"Sounds like you have a problem"* is helpful. Children so often give their power away. They believe that the other child has the problem, so they themselves are powerless to find a solution. They have to wait until the other child changes. This view renders them helpless.

Sometimes children attempt to give their power to the parent. If you rescue them, you take their power. Gradually they begin to doubt their capability and adequacy. They will continue to look to you to solve their problems.

When children realize that *they* own the responsibility for solving their own problems, they take the first step towards resolution. They take responsibility for generating and implementing solutions. They claim their own power and learn, with increasing skill, to live responsibly.

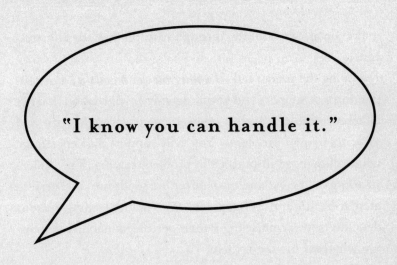

"I know you can handle it."

"If you stay after school to make up the work, you'll miss the band rehearsal. Sounds like you have a tough decision to make. *I know you can handle it.*"
"Both you and Jeremy need to use the computer to finish your homework tonight. That'll take some thought. *I know you can handle it.*"
"This circumstance seems impossible to you? *I know you can handle it.*"

In each of the above situations the parent stated the problem clearly, empathized with the child's feelings, and returned the problem to the child with the phrase *"I know you can handle it."* It is likely that these children felt understood and cared about. They believed they were taken seriously because their parents showed faith in their abilities to make decisions, follow through, and live with the outcomes.

Using the parent talk *"I know you can handle it"* as a routine form of support and encouragement will remind you not to rescue children and to allow them to struggle with and solve their own problems. You will support and encourage while allowing skill practice in problem solving. The understanding of "I can handle whatever life sends me" is crucial to mental health and to happiness. One of the leading reasons that adults seek counseling is their perceived inability to manage whatever life sends them.

We cannot always control the circumstances in our lives, but we must feel secure that we *can* cope with them. *"I know you can handle it"* is parent talk that communicates your respect for the child's ability to manage her own life.

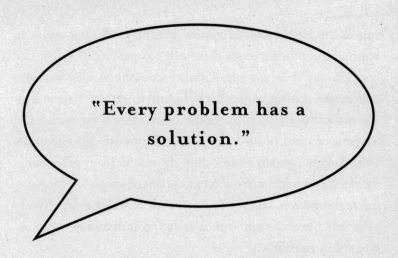

"Every problem has a solution."

Rick has a problem. His science project is due in one week, and he hasn't started it yet. Bonnie has a problem, too. Her best friend just moved to New Jersey, and she feels sad.

How will these children react to their problems? What attitudes, efforts, and resources will they choose? Their reactions may depend on how skillfully you demonstrate your beliefs about problems and the parent talk you use as you discuss them.

Problem solving is made up of skills such as problem identification, brainstorming possible solutions, consensus seeking, weighing alternatives, goal setting, and evaluating. Often children don't possess these skills, so they disown their problems, blame others, lie, or pretend the problem doesn't exist. In addition, they often hold erroneous beliefs that hinder effective problem solving. They believe that they don't have the *ability* to be successful problem solvers.

"Every problem has a solution" is parent talk that will help your children begin to see themselves as problem solvers. Use it often. Say it as you recall and discuss the week's activities and events during your weekly family meetings. Repeat it as you brainstorm with your children possible ways to reduce the amount of mud being tracked into the house. Vocalize it as you struggle to open a stuck desk drawer in front of the family. As your children are increasingly exposed to *"Every problem has a solution,"* they'll come to understand that you firmly believe it. Slowly, it will sink into their minds and be available when they need it.

"Every problem has a solution" must be lived as well as spoken. Children need to see their *parents* demonstrate a belief in this philosophy if *they* are to believe it. If there is a discrepancy between what we say and what we do, children will imitate what we do. Our actions, as well as our words, must demonstrate our belief that every problem has a solution.

When problems occur, make the search for solutions more important than fixing blame and handing out punishment. If someone spills milk, see the situation as an opportunity to model effective handling of a problem. Instead of rushing to find out who did it, focus on finding a solution to the immediate problem. Let your children witness how a mature adult approaches and solves the problem of milk on the carpet. When the crisis is over and the milk is cleaned up, use the incident to model a problem-solving process while producing a solution that will prevent more spills. Help children define the problem, list possible solutions, consider the alternatives, and reach consensus on a solution. Involve them in monitoring the implementation of the plan and evaluating the success of the solution.

Youngsters need to actively experience a problem-solving process many times before it becomes internalized. They must have it explained and modeled for them over and over. You must *use* it in your home if you want them to learn it. Use it for such problems as too many phone calls in the evening, too much complaining about responsibilities, too much litter in the yard. Use the process with a child who continues to forget to take his lunch to school, dominates the family discussion time, or ends up in time-out at school.

When both your actions and your parent talk communicate your belief that *"Every problem has a solution,"* you encourage children to give up helplessness and replace it with confidence in their own skills and abilities. You teach them to interpret the roadblocks of their lives as opportunities to learn and grow. You teach them that instead of complaining and disowning their responsibility for problems, they can face and solve them.

"SURE I KNOW WHAT WOULD SOLVE
THIS PROBLEM. MORE FLOOR SPACE."

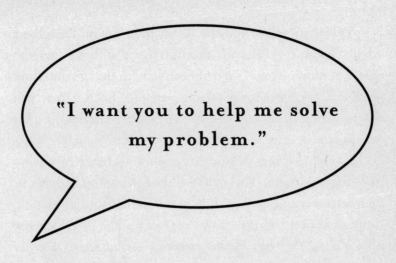

"I want you to help me solve my problem."

Jackie likes to hum while he chews his food. His mother is irritated with the behavior, and it spoils her dinner. She has spoken to him about it several times without much change. She will meet with him privately after dinner to discuss the situation.

The weather is cold when Mary leaves for school in the morning, so she wears a jacket. On her return trip home it is warm, and she leaves the jacket at school. She now has two jackets, two sweaters, and two sweatshirts at school. Her mom will hold a special meeting before bedtime to attempt to find a solution.

Pedro loves the bedtime ritual of lying in the top bunk while his father reads to him and his brother before they get tucked in. He likes the stories so much that he often blurts out his opinions when his dad pauses for a breath. Pedro's father has decided to address the situation in a private conversation.

These parents have many things in common. Each has a child choosing a behavior that interferes with the parent's peace of mind. Each is tired of dealing with the situation, and each has arranged for a private meeting. Each parent will begin the meeting with one of my favorite phrases, *"I want you to help me solve my problem."*

In each of these cases, a one-on-one problem-solving meeting will occur. The child will be confronted with his or her behavior and invited to help the parent find a solution. Important to the success of this approach is the parent's belief that *it is not the child, but the parent himself or herself who has the problem.*

If humming while eating bothers Jackie's mother, then it is the adult who has the problem. If Mary's mom creates stress for herself because her daughter leaves clothes at school, the mom has a problem. If Pedro's dad feels irritated by Pedro's outbursts, again it's the parent who has the problem.

Some adults believe that in examples such as those cited, it's the child who has a problem. After all, they reason, the *child* is the one humming, leaving clothes at school, or inter- rupting the story. The child is the one exhibiting inappropri- ate behavior.

A different point of view, however, is that the humming is not a problem to the youngster. It only irritates the parent. The interruption doesn't bother Pedro. It bothers his father.

While it's certainly true that in each case both the parent and the child will benefit from a change in behavior, it is really the *parent* who has the problem.

If adults enter a problem-solving meeting believing that the child has a problem, they naturally talk and act as if the child is wrong. Even if the words and demeanor are caring and gentle, the child can hardly escape feeling accused. The common reaction is defensiveness and resistance. When children feel pushed, they push back. Now they are unable to genuinely listen to the problem and help to create a solution. The *"You* have a problem stance" has failed.

When adults communicate from the *"I want you to help me solve my problem"* approach, children feel that their input is invited and respected. Cooperation and *mutual* problem solving are encouraged. The child is more likely to understand the adult's problem and less likely to view the parent as an adversary.

When you invite children to help you solve *your* problem, you encourage them to join you in the search for solutions. You ask them to make a personal investment in the problem, which greatly enhances the chances that the problem solving will result in a workable solution.

All three of the parents in the previous examples knew they had problems and invited their children to help them solve those problems. Jackie and her mother agreed that humming would be allowed when Jackie ate alone or in the family room. Pedro and his father created a special hand signal to remind Pedro that he needed to wait before speaking. Just talking seriously with him in this respectful, caring way focused Pedro's attention on the problem, and his behavior changed significantly. Mary and her mom agreed that Mary could leave jackets and sweaters in her locker until Friday, when she would bring all her clothes home.

These parents did indeed have a lot in common. Each helped a child participate in a problem-solving process. Each found a mutually acceptable solution with the youngster without feeling the need to "pull rank." Each modeled effective problem-solving and communication skills, and each discovered the value of the parent talk *I want you to help me solve my problem."*

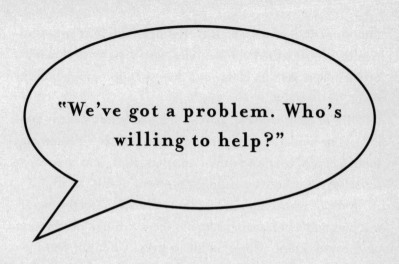

"We've got a problem. Who's willing to help?"

Right now, as you read this page, somewhere a child is spilling milk at the kitchen table. Across the street a similar scene is unfolding. On one side of the street, the parent says, "What's the matter with you? I've warned you not to fill that glass so high. You're spoiling our dinner and ruining the rug at the same time. Go to your room until you can learn to be more careful." The parent who lives across the street, dealing with the same situation, comments, *"We've got a problem. We need a towel and a sponge, quickly. Who's willing to help?"*

Both parents are reacting verbally to a perceived problem. Both are sending their children a message. Unknowingly, both have sent messages much more detailed than their spoken words would indicate.

"What's the matter with you?" sends the child a silent, implied message. The message is, "Rugs and dinner are more important than people and their feelings. This is a blame-and-punishment-oriented family. The best way to deal with a problem here is to fix blame and dole out appropriate punishment."

"We've got a problem" parent talk also sends a silent message. The underlying communication here is, "People and their feelings are more important than rugs, and the search for solutions is how we handle a problem in this family."

Most of what children learn is not taught directly. Significant amounts of learning come to them through observation of the important people in their lives. Children learn by watching, listening, absorbing, and imitating the behaviors and attitudes they see and hear on display before them.

For instance, children rarely receive specific training on how to deal with a problem. They learn more about handling problems by watching how adults deal with them than they do from direct problem-solving instruction. Their predominant learning comes from what they see and hear modeled.

When milk gets spilled at your dinner table, what is modeled? Do your parent talk and accompanying behavior communicate the importance of problem solving or of blame and punishment? Does your choice of language convey that things are more valuable than people or vice versa?

Children present us with a multitude of opportunities to communicate our belief in problem solving or in blame and punishment. They track in dirt, scratch the furniture, wreck the grass, destroy flowers, knock pictures off walls, forget to return our possessions, mark on the walls, rip clothing, break dishes, leave lights on, park their bikes behind the car, leave tools out in the rain, neglect to write down important phone messages, and engage in a few hundred other parent-testing behaviors. What responses do you give to those tests? Are your answers consistent with the beliefs and values you really wish to communicate?

Learned Helplessness

Ten Things to Say to Promote Learned Helplessness in Your Children

1. "Here, let me do that for you."
2. "I'll pay for it this time, but if it happens again you're going to have to suffer the consequences."
3. "I'll talk to your teacher and see if I can get her to change her mind."
4. "It's late, so I'll let it go this time."
5. "I'll fix it for you."
6. "Don't say anything to your father. I'll see if I can convince him for you."
7. "You're not old enough for a _____."
8. "I haven't got time to show you how right now."
9. "That's too complicated [difficult, involved, sophisticated, much trouble]."
10. "It was raining, so I put your bike in the garage."

"Here, let me do that."

"Let me get that for you."
"I'll do it."
"Let me handle that."

Some parents overfunction. They do things for their children so often, their children stop doing those things for themselves. Consistent use of this behavior produces the phenomenon known as "learned helplessness."

Use the language above as a clue. Do you hear yourself using these phrases frequently? Is "Here, let me do that" a regular part of your parent talk? If so, you could be contributing to learned helplessness in your children.

Sometimes parents are in a hurry. Other times they get impatient. Regardless of your motivation, taking over and doing for your child something she could do for herself disempowers her. It encourages her to view herself as incapable. When your out-loud talk is "Let me handle that," your child's self-talk is likely to be "I can't do it right," or "I'm not good enough."

To find out if you contribute to learned helplessness in your family, monitor your behaviors as well as your parent talk. Are you doing things for your children that they could be doing for themselves? Do you do laundry for a teenager? Do you pack your middle schooler's lunch? Do you tie the shoes and zip the coat of a six-year-old? Do you look up phone numbers for your fourth grader? If so, you could be over-functioning. Remember, the more you function, the less your child has to.

For example, no parent needs to do laundry for a teenager. Our job as parents is to teach our children how to do things for themselves. Their job is to do it. We give them a system. They use the system. Young children can be taught to place laundry in the basket. When they're a bit older, their respon-sibility can be to carry their dirty clothes downstairs to the laundry room. A couple of years later they can learn to sort the laundry. Still later, their responsibility could include folding the clothes. By the time they're teenagers, the whole job could belong to them. Parents who *do for* their teens by doing their laundry aren't helping them. They're doing them a disservice.

Certainly it takes an investment of time to wait while the child zips his own coat or ties her own shoes. Yes, it is frequently necessary to do direct teaching so your adolescent can learn the required behaviors of operating the washer and dryer. There are times when it seems that your effort isn't worth the hassle. Keep in mind, though, that whenever you take over and *do for* your child, you create more work for yourself in the long run. If you do something for your child once, no problem. If you do something for your child twice, it's now expected that you'll do it in the future. If you do something a third time, congratulations, you now have a new job.

"You sure are lucky."

There are many expressions in our language that refer to the concept of luck. Some of the more common are *good fortune, chance,* and *coincidence.* Luck-based comments include: "You're jinxed," "What an unfortunate string of events," "I guess it wasn't in the cards," "That's fate."

When you use the language of luck with children, you embellish the myth that luck is at work in their lives. This style of language diminishes their sense of personal power. It gives some outside force (luck) credit for success and failure. It dilutes their understanding of cause and effect and encourages them to disown the role they play in their own success.

Rachael, age six, worked for twenty minutes building a tower of blocks. After several trials and errors, she created a structure that surpassed her own expectation. Excited about the accomplishment, Rachael showed it to her mother. This

parent missed an opportunity to mention Rachael's perseverance, sense of balance, and effort. She nodded admiringly and
said, "You're lucky it's still standing."

Charles spent three nights at the city library. He logged
ten hours poring through the periodical files looking for ref-
erences for his term paper. When he told his father about the
five new sources he found, his father remarked, "You really
lucked out at the library."

"You sure were in the right place at the right time,"
"You're leading a charmed life," "What a coincidence," "You
stumbled onto a good one there" are more examples of the
language of luck. Parents who talk like this encourage their
children to discount the importance of preparation, skill,
effort, and persistence. They disown the power they do have
and give it away to fate, fortune, or coincidence.

Life appears, in one sense, to be an ongoing mixture of
good and bad breaks. Yet, perhaps what happens to us is really
the result of adequate or inadequate preparation, abundance
or lack of skills, recognizing many or few alternatives, and
responding to or disregarding opportunities. How a child
chooses to see opportunities, which opportunities he chooses
to take advantage of, and the skills and preparation that
youngster brings with him are responsible for success.

Drop the language of luck from your parent talk vocabulary and help your family members feel the power, self-
reliance, and control they have in their own lives.

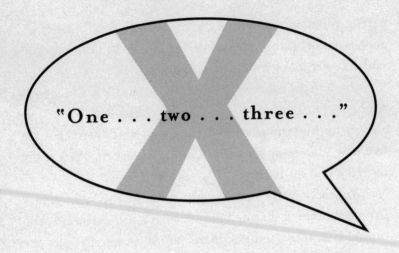

"One . . . two . . . three . . ."

"Billy, please pick up your toys."

"Billy, I asked you to pick up your toys."

"Billy, did you hear me tell you to pick up your toys?"

"Billy, I don't want to have to tell you again to pick up your toys."

"How many times do I have to tell you, Billy, to pick up those darn toys?"

"Billy, you better pick up those toys right this minute."

"I'm not warning you again, Billy, about those toys."

"William Robert, your toys better be picked up before I get in there."

"Okay, this is your last warning about the toys, mister."

"One . . . two . . . three . . ."

Parent talk like this teaches the child only one thing—that he doesn't have to move a muscle until his parent starts counting. Children learn quickly that the parent isn't serious and that nothing of any significance will happen until the words turn to numbers.

The average parent reminds a child nine times before taking action. Regardless of whether the action that follows is skillful or unskillful, nine repetitions of the same request are not necessary. You could take the same action after five repetitions, three, or even one.

When your action follows the ninth request, you teach the child that he can ignore the first eight. When action occurs after the initial request or following one reminder, you communicate your seriousness and establish household norms. The child learns that there won't be numerous reminders.

Some parents are a Number Nine and take action after the ninth invitation. Others are a Number Four and act following the fourth request. Regardless of whether your number is high or low, be assured that your children have your number and they know the odds that number signifies. Even if you're a Two, they know you'll only act every other time. Some children will play those odds. If you're a Seven, more children will risk that you won't take action than would if you were a Two or Three.

In situations like these, let your parent talk reflect the notion that *less is more*. Simply talk less and act more. As you take more action, you'll find you have to talk less. Reduce your number from Nine to Six to Three to One and you'll no longer have a need to say, "One . . . two . . . three . . ."

"I CHOOSE TO LEAVE IT THIS WAY
BECAUSE LEAVING IT THIS WAY IS
A LABOR-SAVING DEVICE."

"There you go again" is a phrase that can have positive or negative effects, depending on how you use it. Some parents use it to point out negative behaviors. "There you go again—forgetting your lunch," or "There you go again—acting moody in the morning."

When used to draw attention to negative actions, "There you go again" is unhelpful. It communicates your negative expectations and verbally reinforces the behavior you desire to eliminate.

This type of parent talk brings what is past into the present, brands the child as "that way," and indirectly encourages both you and the child to project the present behavior into the future.

Since changing the past is impossible, you have locked children into a situation that has no escape. Release children from their past by eliminating mental scorekeeping from your parent talk. If you feel it's necessary to point out negative behaviors, confine your remarks to the present. Focus on what they are doing now.

"There you go again" works like a giant mirror. It's a style of speaking that reflects to children how we see them. It can be used to reflect positively, as well as negatively.

"There you go again—another homework assignment completed on time" is one example of using this phrase in a positive way. It helps the child create a picture in her head of herself as prompt with assignments. *"There you go again—doing more than I required"* encourages the child to picture herself as someone who goes beyond the minimum.

The parent talk you use following *"There you go again"* will give you data on how you're helping your children see themselves. If leadership or honesty or lying or forgetfulness follow, be assured that you are inviting more of the same behavior into your home and into your children's lives.

Create a language assignment for yourself. Use *"There you go again"* in a positive way five times in the next week to highlight those behaviors you want to reinforce in your child. Celebrate as you notice how this phrase is helping your children see themselves in more positive ways. Congratulate yourself as you effectively use language to improve your child's self-esteem.

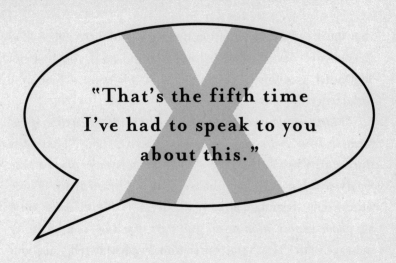

"That's the fifth time I've had to speak to you about this."

"This is the third time you've done that this week."
"That's four—four times you interrupted me while I was speaking."
"This makes three times you've been late for dinner since Sunday."

This kind of parent talk reveals mental scorekeeping. When you keep track of the number of times a behavior has occurred, you take archeological garbage from the past and drag it into the present. The weight of numerous incidents creates strain that prevents you from dealing cleanly with the situation at hand. Scorekeeping builds stress, magnifies the situation, and interferes with the process of communicating clearly and directly.

To step out of the role of scorekeeper, choose parent talk

that speaks as if each situation were new and different. Ask as if you have never asked before. Remind as if you had not reminded previously. Discipline as if this were a first-time occurrence.

"Mary, would you please take your cars off the chair and put them in your bedroom?" is more effective than "That's the third time I've asked, Mary." *"I like it when you're here on time for dinner"* has a greater chance of being heard than "Three times you've been late already this week." *"Please let me finish my phone conversation before you start speaking"* is a healthier message than "That's the fourth time I've had to tell you about that."

Putting a number on the frequency of a behavior focuses the child on the pattern rather than on the specific behavior. It encourages him to see the incident as one in a series of deficient behaviors and to develop a negative picture of himself in his head. The past dragged into the present can easily be projected into the future, setting up a self-fulfilling prophecy.

Monitor your parent talk. Listen for examples of mental scorekeeping. When you hear yourself verbalize a number, *stop*. Dump the historical burden and deliver an honest and clear parent talk interaction that concentrates on the present.

"That's not a good excuse."

Adults often tell children, "That's not a good excuse." By giving them feedback on what we think of their excuses, we believe that we are teaching them to behave more responsibly. Actually, this style of parent talk has the opposite effect.

When we determine the acceptability of a child's excuse, we set ourselves up as judge. We communicate to our children that our role is one of excuse examiner whose job it is to pass judgment on their excuses. That leaves them the role of excuse givers and encourages them to generate excuses for us to rate.

When we say, "That's not a good excuse," we communicate, "If you had a good excuse, I might accept it. If I accept your excuse, then you will be excused from responsibility or consequences." Every time this happens we undermine the child's responsibility and actually invite excuses. Children are thus encouraged to spend their time and energy creating "better" excuses instead of taking action to rectify the situation.

When we use parent talk that accepts or rejects excuses, children see *us* as responsible for the consequences. If we listen to an excuse for an unfinished responsibility and reject it as not good enough, they believe we are the cause of their having to do it over. It we consider and then deny their excuse for coming home late, once again we are seen as responsible for the grounding. They see *us* as having the power to determine whether or not they have to do it over, get grounded, or experience other consequences. They come to believe that *we* are responsible for whether or not each situation turns out the way they want.

I suggest you use parent talk that keeps you from passing judgment on the excuse. Help children own their behavior and assume more responsibility for it by using language that focuses on consequences and on the role children play in creating them.

When your son offers the excuse, "I know I'm late, but my friend needed a ride home," reply, *I'm glad you're here and safe. When you choose to come home after twelve, you choose to spend the next weekend night at home.*" When he informs you the night before that he needs something for school the next day and offers the excuse that he was "real busy the past few days," direct your parent talk to the consequences. *"When you choose to inform me the night before, you choose to go without."* When your daughter begins excuses for being behind in her homework assignments, refuse to get caught up in evaluating the reasons *even when they seem reasonable.* Reply matter-of-factly, *"Missing homework assignments requires make-up work. You've chosen to participate in extra study time this week."*

Children will usually not back off after the first excuse. They will persist in an effort to make you responsible for the outcome. "I couldn't help it," they'll argue. "I just couldn't get it all done. It's not my fault that each teacher gave a long assignment the same day." Resist the temptation to acknowledge the excuse.

Parent talk that refuses to acknowledge excuses sends children helpful messages. They learn that your role is not that of judging excuses and that their behavior is more important to you than excuses. You teach them through experience that even when life seems unfair or seems to deal them a bad hand, *they can handle it.*

It is very important to us, as parents, to feel that we're fair with our children, so we often enter into the excuse game with the positive intention that they feel heard and understood. Paradoxically, it's the parents who "bend over backward" to be fair by hearing excuses and ruling on them who are perceived by children as showing favoritism. Because these parents acknowledge excuses by listening and ruling on them, the child who is ruled against is likely to believe the parent is unfair.

It's important to realize that children will respect parents who set reasonable guidelines and stick to them. Let children know that you're not angry with them for choosing consequences, that you still like them, and that *they* are responsible for their own circumstances. Communicate that to them by choosing parent talk that refuses to acknowledge excuses.

"IF YOU DON'T ACCEPT GOOD EXCUSES, WOULD YOU CONSIDER ONE THAT'S MARGINAL?"

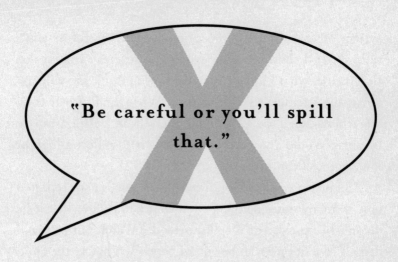

"Be careful or you'll spill that."

"Watch out or you'll fall."
"You'll hurt yourself if you don't slow down."
"That could break if you're not careful."
"That could drop. Be careful."
"Slow down or you'll get a ticket."
"Wear your coat or you'll catch a cold."
"You'll never pass if you don't study."

WARNING: Be careful about giving your children warnings.

Only two things can happen when you give children warnings, and neither is positive. First, warnings can plant doubt in your children's minds. If you consistently show by your parent talk that you doubt a child's ability, that child will eventually begin to doubt herself. Imagine the effect on a child's belief system of hearing many repetitions of "Be careful or you'll fall." After a child has been exposed to several variations on that theme, what kind of thoughts do you think she will create as she attempts to climb a tree? What kind of beliefs do you think she'll develop about herself in relationship to heights? Would you expect her behavior to reflect a high or low degree of confidence?

"Sit up close or you'll spill your food" needs to be repeated only so many times before a child comes to believe that if he doesn't sit up close he'll spill his food. "Watch out or you'll drop it" doesn't need to be voiced very often before the child begins to see himself as a person who is likely to drop things.

Once a child begins to believe he's liable to drop things, it's just a matter of time before he acts out behaviors consistent with his programming. Children who believe they drop things do not act confidently; hence, they are more prone to drop things, which confirms their belief that they are indeed a person who drops things. Eventually, they drop enough things to prove their belief to themselves. Then they drop more things.

Warnings take the form of expectations in disguise. Parents who warn children about spilling milk communicate that they expect them to spill milk. Adults who warn youngsters about breaking things send the message that they expect them to break things. After repeated warnings, many children develop expectations of themselves in line with the expressed expectations of others. In time, they learn to expect to spill food and break things.

A second problem with warnings occurs when our warnings do not match the child's experience. We say "Don't run or you'll get hurt." The child runs and she doesn't get hurt. Our parent talk is "Don't climb too high or you'll fall." She climbs high and she doesn't fall. We tell her "If you don't wear your coat, you'll catch a cold." She takes her coat off the instant she's out of our sight and guess what? She doesn't catch a cold. There is only one thing an intelligent child can conclude under these circumstances: We don't know what the heck we're talking about.

When we issue many warnings to our young children that don't match with their experience, they begin to doubt us and our wisdom. They stop taking our warnings seriously. Later, when we warn about the critical issues of promiscuous sex or the dangers of drugs and alcohol, they have stopped listening to our warnings. Previously, they ran and didn't get hurt. They climbed high and didn't fall. Why would our warnings about sex, drugs, or alcohol be any different to them? We lose valuable credibility in the minds of our children just when we need it most.

Be careful of parent talk that issues indiscriminate warnings. An overabundance of cautionary language will attract more of what we are warning about into our children's lives or it will not fit with their experience base and thus erode our credibility in their minds.

Praise, Criticism, and Self-Esteem

"You did a good job."

Praise is the number-one behavior modification tool employed by educators and parents alike. Teachers tell us that praise motivates students, builds self-confidence, and improves self-esteem. The assumption is that praise is helpful. Yet, what if it is a false assumption? Perhaps praise is not always the esteem builder we have believed.

"You did a *good* job" is one example of *evaluative* praise. Others include:

> "You're a *terrific* speller."
> "That's a *beautiful* picture."
> "I think it's *wonderful*."
> *"Fantastic!"*

Evaluative praise evaluates. When you praise someone

with this type of parent talk, you rate them with words like *good, excellent, super, tremendous, fantastic,* and *superb.* In each case your words represent a judgment of what you think about the other person. Your praise is a judgmental interpretation of their behavior, accomplishments, ideas, appearance, character, effort, or energy.

Some parents protest, "Yes, but evaluative praise helps children feel *good!* What's wrong with that?"

Evaluative praise helps the person being praised to feel good *temporarily.* In that sense, it works very much like a drug. It helps people feel good for the moment—and leaves them longing for more. Children are especially susceptible to the dependency induced by heavy doses of evaluative praise.

A frustrated art teacher once explained how she tried to wean praise-dependent children off evaluative praise by describing and appreciating their work. A child would finish a project, bring it to her, and initiate the following discussion:

Student: "How do you like my picture? Is it good?"
Teacher: *"I appreciate the diversity of your design."*
Student: "But is it good?"
Teacher: *"Tell me what you think about it."*
Student: "I like it, but I want to know if it's good."

The above conversation is not atypical. It occurs continually in classrooms or homes, initiated by children hooked on evaluative praise and looking for a quick fix. These children have learned to depend on others for their measures of success. They see others as the major source of approval in their lives, and they have come to "need" a regular shot of evaluative praise to maintain their sense of worth. They want others to tell them they are good, excellent, beautiful, or wonderful.

Without the constant reminders, evaluative praise-dependent youngsters are uncomfortable and insecure. They don't know how to praise themselves. Excessive use of evaluative praise has reinforced a tendency to look away from themselves for evidence of their competence. They cannot enjoy an accomplishment unless somebody is around to approve of it. They rely on others for proof of their importance and ability and do not develop an adequate internal standard of self-worth. Evaluative praise encourages children to take their self-image from others' perceptions and to become dependent on someone else's opinion or approval.

The art teacher in the previous anecdote *can* succeed in weaning her students from evaluative praise, but it will take time and perseverance. Parents looking for ways to help their children develop self-confidence, self-esteem, and self-motivation will not find evaluative praise helpful. The alternatives I suggest are *descriptive* and *appreciative* praise. (See pp. 123–128.)

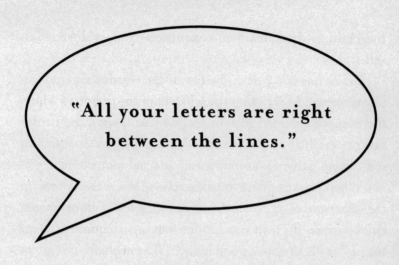

"All your letters are right
between the lines."

This parent talk is an example of *descriptive* praise. Descriptive praise describes accomplishments or situations and affirms the child rather than evaluates what he has done. Other examples are:

> "The floor is clear of toys and clothes. I don't see
> one thing out of place."
> "You worked on that for over an hour. I see you got
> two pages completed."
> "The grass is trim and even. Every blade has been
> chopped off and cleaned up."

Notice the absence of evaluation in descriptive praise. You won't find words like *good, excellent,* or *great.* Descriptive praise simply describes the situation and allows the child to draw his own conclusions and evaluate himself.

Praise has two parts. The first is the words that are actually spoken. The second is the self-talk of the person to whom the praise is directed. It's the second part—what the person says to herself about the praise—that has the greatest effect on self-esteem, self-responsibility, and internal motivation.

When parents praise descriptively—*"You made six trips up the stairs with those boxes of books"*—they leave room for the child to draw his own conclusions. He says to himself, "I am strong" or "I sure am a good helper." The evaluation is internal and is given by a person the child believes: himself. When the praise is believed, self-esteem goes up.

When children develop an internal standard of excellence, they can then judge their own efforts against that standard. Knowing internally what excellence is at home or at school, they are more likely to achieve it. They become more self-directed.

If you want to help your child develop an internal standard of excellence, praise descriptively, leaving the evaluation to the child. When you hear yourself saying (or see yourself writing) "good job," ask yourself: Just what is good about it? Are things in place? Is it accurate? What is it, specifically, about this effort that I think is good? Then use parent talk to communicate your observations descriptively.

Resist saying "excellent" when you look at the dinner table your son arranged. Say instead, *"Every utensil is in the correct place. You got it exactly."* Drop "very good" from your parent talk when commenting on how your daughter cleaned your car. Use descriptive praise such as, *"I don't see one spot of dirt. My car sparkles!"*

Monitor your children's reactions to your new style of praising. Watch their expressions as they tell *themselves,* "I did a good job," "My report was good," and "My effort was superb." Realize that your skillful parent talk with your children has a positive impact on their lives.

"I appreciate your efforts.
Thanks."

Appreciative praise is a form of parent talk that is more empowering than evaluative praise. This alternative language tells the child what behaviors are helpful, explains any positive effects, and shares appreciation.

"*Thank you* for offering to help rake the leaves. That takes a load off my back."
"I was happy to see the sink cleaned out. Now I don't have to do it before I relax. *Thanks.*"

With appreciative praise, the parent makes a statement and the child is able to draw her own conclusion. For example, the parent says, "*Thank you for sweeping the garage. That saved me ten minutes.*" The youngster concludes, "I really helped out." The parent talk is, "*Your help with the computer enabled me to get my budget finished. Thanks!"* The child's self-talk is "I can make a difference. I'm worthwhile." In each case the parent's words leave room for the child to make the evaluation.

When using appreciative praise, it's important to comment on specific acts. If you tell children that you appreciate their honesty, dependability, or promptness, go on to describe specifically the ways in which they acted dependably, honestly, or promptly. A comment like *"I appreciate you being here exactly when you said you would"* allows the youngster to say to herself, "I am dependable."

Begin to strengthen your praise by paying attention to how you verbalize it. Examine the comments you write on notes to your children. When you feel tempted to evaluate, ask yourself, How can I arrange my words so they can draw their own conclusions? How can I arrange my parent talk so the child can evaluate himself?

The act of praising is a skill. It can be developed *and* improved. Remember to praise yourself appreciatively as you accurately acknowledge and describe your children's efforts.

Ten Things to Say to Share Appreciation

1. "Thank you for _____."
2. "I appreciate it that _____."
3. "That saved me a half hour of my day. Thanks."
4. "Your efforts made things a lot easier for me."
5. "I really needed your help. Thanks for being there for me."
6. "That put a big smile on my face."
7. "You really helped our family when _____."
8. "We all benefited from your efforts with _____."
9. "I'm feeling really loved right now."
10. "I feel honored that you _____."

"That's terrible."

Criticism and praise are closely related. They're flip sides of the same coin. Criticism, like praise, can be delivered in evaluative, descriptive, or appreciative terms. *Terrible, ugly, sloppy, poor, disgusting,* and *awful* are examples of criticism that evaluates. Evaluative criticism ("Your clean-up job was terrible" or "That's a poor effort"), like evaluative praise, gives the child little useful information. It's not helpful for the child to know that the clean-up job was terrible unless he knows specifically *why* you think so. It's of little benefit for the youngster to know her effort was poor unless she knows exactly *what* was poor. Without specific knowledge, a child cannot correct mistakes or learn from them.

If you tell your son that the shovel needs to be hosed off and dried before it's put away, you give him information he can use to improve his clean-up effort. When you show your daughter the dirt behind the boxes, she'll know why you thought the end product was poor. When you're *descriptive* with your parent talk, giving specific information about what you dislike and why, the child has valuable information from which to learn. However, if your comments are evaluative, the child is left wondering what it was that wasn't good enough.

Sharing displeasure or giving information about what you would appreciate in the future is another way to give children specific feedback. For example:

> "I don't like cleaning up the sink when I get home.
> I would appreciate it if the brushes are cleaned
> out and put away next time."
> "I'd appreciate glasses being put in the dishwasher."
> "I like it best when you leave the living room the way
> you found it before you used it. Books belong on the
> shelf, and toys belong in the box."

Children generally respond better when you share what you would appreciate or describe what you do not like than they do if you criticize with evaluation. You'll get a more positive response by stating *"Empty milk cartons belong in the garbage can. I don't enjoy seeing them left in the refrigerator,"* than you will by saying "This refrigerator is a mess." You will encourage greater cooperation when your remark is *"I don't enjoy being interrupted,"* than when you say "You're rude and inconsiderate."

Children often hear feedback that evaluates as an attack. They believe it is aimed directly at them and they take it personally. Resentment, resistance, and defensiveness follow. If you learn to use parent talk that speaks to the situation instead of the person and mention *what* was done rather than *who* did it, there is less chance that children will take offense. Choose words that focus on what was or was not accomplished, what is included or is missing from your expectation, what you specifically like or dislike.

"*There is grass on the patio and sidewalk that needs to be swept back into the yard*" focuses on the grass-cutting responsibility and specifically describes the problem. "You did a lousy job" draws attention to the person and does not offer instruction. "It's ten-fifteen, and the meeting has started" speaks to the situation. "You're late" points to the person. "You forgot to put gas in the car" puts the spotlight on the person. "*The gas gauge is below the agreed-upon level*" points to the problem.

Listen to your criticism. Become increasingly aware of the parent talk you use to communicate negative feedback to children. When you hear yourself evaluating, stop. Recall the rules of criticism: *Speak to the situation and describe it specifically.* Rephrase your negative feedback. Choose parent talk that will educate rather than evaluate.

"Next time . . ."

"*Next time,* please wipe the peanut butter and jelly off the
counter before you go out to play."
"*Next time,* please wait until I'm off the phone before you
begin talking."
"*Next time,* ask in a soft voice."

"*Next time*" is a useful piece of parent talk that will help to
plant positive pictures in your child's head of what you want
to have happen in the future. The words you use to follow this
sentence starter focus the child's attention on what you expect
and enable her to picture the positive outcome of your desire
rather than the negative behavior you wish to eliminate.

Adding the phase "*next time*" to your parent talk doesn't
guarantee your child will choose the desired behavior at the
next opportunity. But it does increase your odds that the

behavior will occur. If nothing else, it helps you add positive phrasing to your style of parent talk.

"*Next time,* use your indoor voice" is more positive than "Don't be so loud!"
"*Next time,* take your shoes off inside the door" is a friendlier way of speaking than "Don't track mud in here."
"*Next time,* finish chewing before you begin talking" plants a more positive picture than "Don't talk with your mouth full!"

When you use *"next time"* as a positive alternative to the word *don't,* you activate the child's subconscious mind to work in your behalf. Consider the following:

As you read this paragraph, don't think of a large blue elephant. Now, don't see that large blue elephant sitting on a park bench eating an ice cream cone. What happened? If you're like most of the participants who attend my parent or teacher workshops, you've created some picture of a large blue elephant in your mind. This phenomenon explains why "don't" is largely ineffective with children. The subconscious mind doesn't hear the word "don't."

When you tell a child "Don't run," what is the picture she sees in her mind? Running. What word stands out and makes an impression? "Run." When you say "Don't be late," the words and the picture that enter the mind are, "Be late." When you tell a child "Don't forget," you're actually sending that child instructions to "forget." When your parent talk includes the word *don't,* you are strengthening the exact behavior you wish to eliminate.

The phrase *"next time"* not only plants a positive picture in the subconscious mind, it also concentrates on teaching. The words that follow *"next time"* instruct. By describing the desired behavior, you give children useful information they can use later.

"Next time, walk around Kristin's blocks on your way outdoors" is instructive and communicates the new behavior. *"Next time,* let me know a few days in advance that you need these supplies for school" teaches by making your expectations clear.

Are you interested in developing a style of communication that gives your children clear instructions as to your expectations? Do you want them to create positive pictures of desired behaviors? Then, next time, strengthen your parent talk with the phrase *"next time."*

Parent Talk at
Its Worst

The Twenty Worst Things to Say
to Your Child

1. "We never wanted you anyway."
2. "If you don't stop that, I'm going to leave you here."
3. "You're the reason we're getting a divorce."
4. "Why can't you be more like your brother [sister]?"
5. "Children should be seen and not heard."
6. "Because I said so, that's why."
7. "I wish I never had you."
8. "If you do that, then you're not my son [daughter]."
9. "If you don't stop crying, I'll give you something to cry about."
10. "Here, let me do that for you."
11. "I can't stand you."
12. "Stop being so _____ [stupid, lazy, smart-mouthed, picky, etc.]."
13. "You're useless [sick, disgusting, revolting, etc.]."
14. "Then I guess you'd better get a different mommy."
15. "You make me sick."
16. "Where are your brains?"
17. "What's wrong with you?"
18. "Watch your mouth."
19. "You'll never amount to anything good."
20. "Just try it, buddy."

"If you don't straighten up,
I'm going to leave you here."

Parents use this phrase in a misguided attempt to get their children to behave. It is usually uttered in a public place by a parent who feels unempowered and is unable to get a child to behave in a certain way. Feeling powerless or embarrassed, the parent resorts to a combination of threat and scare tactic: "If you don't stop that, I'm going to leave you here."

All children have abandonment fears. A young child's worst fear is that a parent will leave him or her and that he or she won't be safe. Please refrain from threatening children with this frightening piece of parent talk.

One alternative is to use your parent talk skills to give your child a choice. Instead of scaring your son with "I'll leave you here" language, tell him *"Brian, if you keep choosing that behavior, we're going home. If you choose to talk in a normal voice, we'll stay and shop. You decide."* Or tell your daughter directly what you want. *"Cecile, I want you to ask in a normal voice. Whining doesn't work with me."*

A third alternative is to stop and take a break. The "I'm going to leave you here" phrase is a signal that one or both of you is tired and may need a nap. *"Jerry, let's sit over here and rest for a while. It sounds like both of us could use a time-out."*

Regardless of the reason for its use or its level of effectiveness, "I'll leave you here" parent talk is unacceptable. Please make a different choice.

"Why can't you be more like your sister?"

"Your brother never acted like that."
"Your sister would have finished that by now."
"Your brother got all A's in ninth grade."

When parents compare siblings, someone is shown to be deficient. This style of parent talk sends a message to the child with the perceived deficiency that she's not enough. She's not smart enough, fast enough, thorough enough, or good enough. Repetitive use of the *not good enough* message settles into a child's mind and over time becomes a core belief. Once the belief becomes internalized, the child, through her behaviors and attitudes, proves and reproves that belief to herself and to those around her.

In addition to conveying to the child that she's not good enough, this type of parent talk has another drawback. Comparisons increase sibling rivalry. When parents compare siblings, feelings of separateness increase and the relationship between the youngsters is damaged. This intensifies natural sibling rivalry and creates more hassles for parents.

Instead of comparisons, use parent talk that focuses on descriptions of the behavior you desire and the potential for improvement. *"How can we help you work faster?"* will achieve better results than, "Your brother would have been done by now." *"Your room does not meet the family cleanliness standard. The under-the-bed area needs work"* will be more effective than, "I never had to speak to your sister about her room."

To drop comparisons from your language patterns, you must be able to accept each child in your family for the person he is. Each is unique. Each has strengths and personal edges he needs to grow along. Help your children see the beauty of their own uniqueness by focusing on each individual without the use of comparisons.

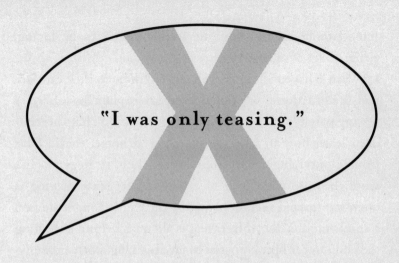

"I was only teasing."

"I was just kidding."
"I didn't really mean it."
"I was only joking around."

A good rule of thumb regarding this area of parent talk is: *If you don't mean it, don't say it.* Calling children names, making fun of them, and teasing has no place in loving families. The parent's job is to love, nourish, and support the child, not be cute and clever with put-downs disguised as humor.

Humorous put-downs are seldom funny to the recipient. More often, youngsters take them seriously and come to believe major portions of them. Look closely at the cost and determine if it's worth the payoff.

"But I didn't intend to be mean," a mother told me at one of my evening workshops. She was probably right. She didn't intend to be mean. And she didn't intend to be loving, either.

"But I have to toughen up my children so they can face real-life situations," one father argued to explain his pattern of teasing parent talk. He reasoned that if he didn't help his children learn how to take some teasing at home, they'd have trouble surviving away from home. This strategy doesn't work, because what feels to a parent like gentle teasing is often interpreted as humiliation by the child. Toughening up a child emotionally with teasing is about as helpful as beating the child to get him prepared to face the neighborhood bully.

Let the world do the job of toughening up. Eliminate teasing and humorous put-downs from your parent talk and concentrate on your main job: providing a haven where love and support predominate.

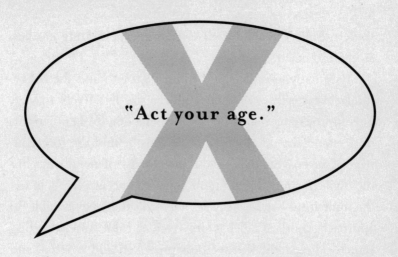

"Act your age."

Patty couldn't seem to make up her mind what color construction paper she wanted for her rainy day art project. She took orange, then changed to blue, and finally decided on red. Then, when she noticed her brother had green, she was sure *she* wanted that color. Her mom relented, exchanging red for green, and Patty pouted because her brother got green first. She began to cry. In exasperation, Patty's mother chided, "Act your age!"

Actually, Patty *was* acting her age. Developmental characteristics of six-year-olds include ambivalence, stubbornness, and frequent tears. Patty is being reprimanded for acting like a six-year-old. She can hardly miss the irritation and rejection in her mother's words. Her *self* is being attacked. By not accepting the child that Patty actually is, by struggling against understandable, *normal* six-year-old behaviors, her mother is undermining the child's self-esteem and is creating needless stress for herself.

Parents who understand human growth and the behavioral characteristics of their children are less likely to view age-appropriate behavior as misbehavior. When parents understand the developmental reasons behind the forgetfulness of seven-year-olds or the put-downs of preadolescents, they will be more accepting of children and less likely to use the unhelpful *"Act your age."* It will then be possible to approach children's behaviors from a calm and accepting stance. The parent will feel less provoked and stressed, and more able to respond with warmth and understanding.

"Act your age" hints that the child's behavior is somehow unacceptable. Parents use it with positive intentions to help children learn that what they're doing is not appropriate. Yet the parent talk of "Act your age" is too general and vague to teach the child when behaviors *are* appropriate. If parents want certain behaviors to manifest and others to disappear, they must accept the child where he or she is at that moment while suggesting and encouraging specific behavioral alternatives.

"Patty, do eenie-meenie to help you decide" is language that gives Patty an option to consider. *"It's hard to choose sometimes, isn't it?"* communicates acceptance while helping the child get in touch with her feelings.

"Act your age" does not instruct or help the child understand what behaviors are expected. Instead, it communicates disrespect and misunderstanding. If you wish to make your language congruent with a desire to nurture children, eliminate *"act your age"* from your parent talk.

"What did I just tell you?"

"Haven't you started yet?"
"Didn't I just explain that?"
"Do you know where your bedroom is?"
"Where were you when I went over this?"

Such inquiries fall into a category of communication called Questions to Which the Parent Already Knows the Answer. This type of parent talk is a thinly veiled accusation that requires no answer. It is delivered to express displeasure and often smacks of sarcasm and ridicule. If children do answer one of these questions, they are often seen as disrespectful.

In reality, asking questions to which you already know the answer begins the exchange of disrespect. Can you imagine asking a neighbor, "Didn't I just explain that, Howard?" or "Mrs. Shafer, haven't you started yet?" Our language reveals the level of respect we extend to others. By eliminating these questions from our parent talk repertoire, we can model respect for all people, regardless of their age or status.

When you hear yourself asking questions of this nature, halt. Ask a different kind of question, this one of yourself. Ask yourself, What is my motivation for asking this question? Examine your answer. If the purpose of your question is to communicate anger or irritation, drop the question and state your irritation openly. *"I'm angry about having to explain this twice,"* or *"I'm irritated that I have to stop my activity to see if you got started."*

Is your intention to remind your children to go to their bedroom, get started, or pay more careful attention during your explanation? If so, tell them directly. *"Terry, please go to your bedroom now." "Jasmine, please begin the dishes."*

Watch out for questions that require no answer. You may be about to begin the cycle of disrespect.

Fifteen Things Parents Say to Guilt-Trip Their Children

1. "You ought to be ashamed of yourself."
2. "Someone who loves their father [mother] never would have done that."
3. "Jesus wouldn't like that."
4. "What will the neighbors think?"
5. "You should know better."
6. "That'll make me feel bad."
7. "And you call yourself a Christian [Jew, Methodist, Baptist, etc.]."
8. "You've disappointed me and your father."
9. "If you do that, you'll hurt my feelings."
10. "You're giving me a headache."
11. "I'm glad your dead grandfather isn't here to see this."
12. "You're going to be the death of me. Then you'll be sorry."
13. "God sees everything you do."
14. "If you do that, I'll never forgive you."
15. "I can't sleep at night worrying about you."

All of these expressions are an attempt to create guilt in the heart of the recipient. Their use flows from a belief that people must feel guilty before they will change. It's an effort to elicit a desired behavior through manipulation and control. The idea is that if the other person can be shamed into feeling guilty, they'll change their behavior and do what we desire.

There are times when shaming works and produces the behavior we want from our children. But at what price? Along with shame and guilt come the core beliefs of "I'm no good," "I'm not enough," "I'm wrong," "I can never do anything right," "I'm not worthwhile," or "No one likes me." These aren't the kind of Life Sentences that most parents want their children believing and acting out in their homes. Yet these core beliefs are exactly what parents create in their children when they choose a style of parent talk that shames youngsters into feeling guilty.

Children who are shamed regularly come to believe that the shame is justified, that they must have earned it and deserve it. They *see* themselves as shameful, begin to *believe* they are shameful, and then *act* in accordance with those beliefs. This negative belief system tends to attract increased shaming from the significant adults in their lives, which reinforces their negative core beliefs. These children get caught up in a self-renewing cycle of behaviors and parental responses that is difficult to exit.

The alternative to shaming children is a style of parent talk that is open, honest, and direct. Present choices to them. Explain what happens if they choose a certain behavior and what happens if they don't. Allow them to choose, and follow through with the legitimate consequences of those actions. Children learn from caring adults who help them to evaluate their choices and the results that follow.

If you have strong feelings about a behavior or desired response, tell the child directly. Explain the reasons for your feelings.

Communicate honestly without sneaking guilt into the

equation in an effort to manipulate. Refuse to be one of those parents who cause children to feel shame and guilt for their actions.

Shame and guilt often backfire. Their use produces resistance and resentment. Children realize on some level that they're being manipulated, pushed, and controlled by parent talk that shames. Manipulation breeds resentment. Pushing calls forth pushing back. Control is resented.

Step out of the resistance-resentment cycle by telling children directly what you expect and why. *"I'm angry about the broken window and you'll need to find a way to pay for it"* is more effective than "You should have known better." *"Looks like you've chosen summer school again this summer. The two D's will have to be made up on your time"* is healthier than the guilt-laying "You've really disappointed us with this report card." *"I'm furious about this situation. Fists are not a way we settle things in this family"* is a truer statement than "I wonder what your dead grandfather would think if he could see you now."

Shame and guilt are not congruent with a parent talk philosophy that focuses on mutual respect and honesty. Use the techniques presented throughout this book to replace language patterns that foster shame and guilt. Stay centered in your efforts to create respectful, responsible children by modeling those attributes in your behaviors and in your parent talk.

"We never wanted you anyway."

"I can't stand you."
"I wish I never had you."
"You're disgusting."
"You make me sick!"
"You'll never amount to anything good."
"You're the reason we're getting a divorce."

This kind of parent talk is inexcusable. Regardless of what your child has done, no matter what his or her tone of voice, these parental responses are totally inappropriate. They are an indication of only one thing. You are out of control, and it's time to put yourself in time-out.

These are vicious words that wound the spirit and slash the soul. They are a signal to you that something is more than amiss in your parent-child relationship. When you hear these words come out of your mouth, it is time to take a break and do some serious self-examination.

Immediately remove yourself from the situation. Go for a walk. Take a hot bath. Jump on a bicycle and start pedaling. Get someone to watch your children so you can go to a movie, exercise, or get away for the weekend. Rake the yard, shovel snow, or wash the car. Go to church, read a book, or call a friend. Give yourself and your child the time and space necessary to cool off and regain perspective.

Long term, it's time to consider counseling for you, your child, and the family. "I wish I never had you" and "You make me sick" reveal a drastic situation that calls for serious remedies. If this type of parent talk has become a pattern in your life, please get some help now. Turn to a counselor, member of the clergy, or school personnel. Do it now. You and your children are worth it.

Intimacy

Ten Things to Say to Build Family Solidarity

1. "How about a game of checkers [Monopoly, cards, Scrabble, etc.]?"
2. "It's time for a family meeting. Let's gather around the kitchen table."
3. "It's bedtime. Who would like a story?"
4. "Now that we've cleaned the garage together, let's all go get an ice cream cone."
5. "Jenny, how about you and I go for a walk [ride in the car, bike ride]? I haven't had a chance to touch base with you for a while."
6. "Come here and let me rub your back."
7. "Let's put that in our family history file. It'll help us remember what we enjoyed doing together at this time in our lives."
8. "Whose turn is it to write in the family journal?"
9. "Let's set some goals for the coming year. What do we really want to accomplish as a family?"
10. "Bill, please turn off the TV now. It's *Prime Time*."

The single biggest detriment to family solidarity continues to be parents' unwillingness to turn off the television. This lost time, often spent with inappropriate amounts of exposure to violence, sexuality, and an endless bombardment of commercials, could be better filled with family activity that produces feelings of connectedness and belonging. Turn the television off and use your parent talk to begin conversations and activities to get the family working, playing, and talking together. *Prime time* is *family time*.

"USE MY MIND? AT HOME?"

"I love you."

I never heard the words *"I love you"* from my mother. She showed her love by cooking, washing, and picking up after me. She worked for hours producing elaborate cross-stitch, quilts, and wall hangings. She kept score at every Little League game I ever played in. She attended *all* my high school athletic events. I know my mother loved me. Yet I never heard her say the words aloud.

After my mom's death, my dad developed cancer and was given only months to live. I made a decision that he wasn't making his transition into another life until I heard the words *"I love you"* from his lips. I set out to teach him how to say them.

Every time I visited my dad or talked to him on the phone, I ended the encounter with *"I love you."* I figured that after a few repetitions from me, he'd respond with "I love you, too."

But he wouldn't or couldn't use those three words I wanted so badly to hear. I'd say *"I love you,"* and he'd respond with "Okay" or "All right."

I persisted with modeling *"I love you"* language for several months before the first breakthrough. One day, Dad took a step closer by responding to my declaration of love with "Me, too." Over the next several weeks he used a number of variations of "Me, too." They included "Same here," "Same for me," and "Ditto." He could say "Me, too" if I told him I loved him, but he couldn't quite get over the hump to say "I love you" directly.

What my dad and mom didn't realize was that having loving feelings or acting lovingly are different than saying *"I love you."* I, like any child (or adult), need to experience love in many modes, and that includes hearing the words.

Some children are tactile and need to be touched to *feel* loved. Others are visual and need to *see* demonstrations of our love. Still others are auditory and need to *hear* the words. Why not show your children all three variations of *"I love you"*?

Make *"I love you"* a regular part of your parent talk. Say it often and accompany it with a hug, a smile, or a wink.

Let *"I love you"* stand alone. It can be a complete sentence and deserves to be treated as such.

"I love you, but . . ." is usually followed by a concern, problem, or frustration. When we express our love along with concerns, we send a mixed message. Children get confused and conclude that the love part is a manipulation intended to soften them up before the real message is delivered.

When you add a condition to your love—"I love you when you smile like that" or "I love you when you choose that happy mood"—your parent talk communicates that your love is conditional. Children hear "I only love you when . . ." To love unconditionally, say *"I love you"* without any condition attached.

My dad lived a year longer than anyone expected. During that time we created an intimacy and connectedness that had not been previously present in our relationship. Still, I was about to give up on hearing *"I love you."* I toyed with the idea of just telling him what I wanted from him. I resisted because I felt it would somehow be better if it came without asking.

Three months before Dad's death, I ended a telephone conversation that included talk on baseball, family, and weather with my now familiar sign-off, *"I love you."* There was a pause at the other end of the line. Then came the sweetest parent talk I have ever heard, sent by a seventy-seven-year-old man to his fifty-four-year-old son: *"I love you, too."*

"Sally, Charles, Roberto, Mary, Helene, Pedro, Sam, William, Megan, Jennifer, Claris, Ernie, Danielle, Anthony, Harry, Nancy"

The sweetest sound in any language is the sound of your own name. Names get our attention, build connectedness, and help us to bond. For those reasons, make your children's names an integral part of your parent talk.

Use their names at the beginning of a sentence.

> "*Bonnie,* would you get that for me, please?"
> "*Germaign,* I'd like some help with this."
> "*Debbie,* did you make that call already?"

Use children's names in the middle of a sentence.

> "That's what I wanted, *Bobby,* to happen with that."
> "I don't understand, *Gina,* how that occurred."
> "I guess, *Brenda,* I'll have to do it over."

Names can also be used at the end of a sentence.

"I like the way that turned out, *Victor.*"
"Are you satisfied with the results, *Nolan?*"
"I'm leaving now, *Alexis.*"

Some children only hear their own name when a parent is angry. "I told you, *John Robert,* never to use that language in this house," or "*Karen Marie,* get in here right now!" In those cases, the name sounds like a weapon being used against the owner.

It is important that names be used with warmth and kindness. Use them to show interest, communicate caring, and extend love to every member of your family. Intimacy increases as a result of parent talk that includes the positive use of names.

There are two other words that create such intense intimacy that parents seldom use them. They are the words *son* and *daughter.* "I enjoyed your reaction to that, *Son,*" or "Hey, *Daughter,* let's go for a walk," are examples of using those words effectively.

Add the words *son* and *daughter* to your parent talk and watch what happens. Notice your feelings and the reactions you get from others. Monitor your comfort level to see how you react to the use of these two important words.

"I noticed."

"*I noticed* you like to wear red."
"*I noticed* you have a new friend."
"*I noticed* you haven't been talking on the phone lately."

"*I noticed* . . ." is parent talk that communicates to the child, "I see you. You are important here. You are visible to me. I notice you." Everyone likes to be noticed. Being noticed builds self-esteem. As parents, it is our job to help our children realize that we see them. It's a way we communicate to the child that he is valued and appreciated.

Use parent talk to notice your child's learning.

"*I see* you're learning to tell time."
"You just divided that in half. We call that fractions.
Did you know you were learning fractions?"

"You just listed four things you need to do and picked
one to start on. That's called 'setting priorities.'
You're learning about time management."

Children aren't always aware that they are learning. By
pointing out their learning we help them create pictures in
their heads of themselves as learners. They begin to think and
believe, "I am a learner." Once that belief is in place, they *act*
more like learners. Learning then increases, which strengthens their belief that "I am a learner."

When you use the parent talk phrase *"I noticed . . ."*
descriptions are preferable to evaluations. The idea is to communicate to your child that you notice her, not to evaluate,
rate, or judge her. Refrain from parent talk that gives an
appraisal of your child's effort, energy, product, or behavior.

Examples of evaluative *"I noticed . . ."* statements include:

"*I see* you did a good job on that."
"*I noticed* you were wonderful with your brother."
"*I saw* the excellent way you played defense."

Examples of descriptive *"I noticed . . ."* statements include:

"*I noticed* you're learning to be a writer."
"*I saw* that you made up with your sister following
the argument."
"*I see* that you've been getting up in time to enjoy
your breakfast."

Add "I noticed . . ." to your parent talk and to your self-talk. Tell yourself, "I noticed you've been implementing these parent talk phrases on a consistent basis," or "I noticed the positive effect this style of speaking is having on my children." If you haven't noticed your implementation efforts, why not begin with *"I noticed . . ."*?

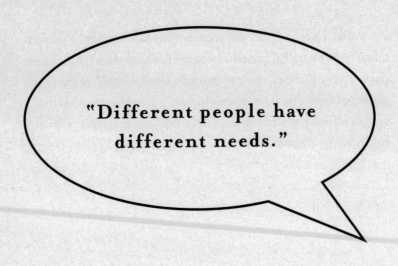

"Different people have different needs."

"Jeremy gets to go to the library. That's not fair."
"Alice doesn't have to work with a math tutor and I do.
It's not fair."
"How come Danielle got some new clothes? It's not fair."

"That's not fair" is a common childhood complaint. It is an outgrowth of the myth that all children should be treated equally. Children and parents who buy into the equality myth confuse "equality" with "equity."

Equity means that all children have comparable opportunities to be loved, appreciated, and educated. All are entitled to a consistent standard of experiences in the home environment. Equity does *not* mean that all children should be treated the same. No two children *are* the same, and there is no reasonable rationale for treating them that way. We would never deny glasses to a child with poor vision, but should we put glasses on every child? Will they be equal then? Of course not! The intent is that each child see clearly. Some need glasses. Some do not. *Different people have different needs.*

Jeremy gets to go to the library because he needs a book for a research project at school. Alice doesn't work with a math tutor because she's not behind in math. Danielle got new clothes because she outgrew her old ones. Each case is unique and personal. Each requires that children be treated differently.

"Different people have different needs" is parent talk that will help your children understand that "fair" means more than everyone doing the same thing the same way at the same time. You teach them that "fair" means getting what they need when they need it. They learn that "fair" is really tolerance and respect for differences among people.

People are equal only according to law. The home is not about enforcing the law but about helping children create themselves as thinking, tolerant, compassionate, loving *individuals.* Every child really is different and deserves to have those differences accepted and respected. Every parent has the responsibility to address those differences so children can learn and grow maximally. When parents seek to meet the different needs of different children, *everyone* is special, because differences are the norm. As your children develop their own unique potentials, they can be guided and served by the tolerance, wisdom, and fairness of the phrase *"Different people have different needs."*

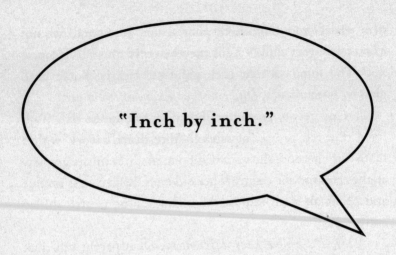

"Inch by inch."

Human development is an orderly growth process that consists of a series of tasks to be confronted and mastered. At the physical level we can say simply that one learns to crawl before walking and learns to walk before running. Each task involves much playful practice and experimentation. Growth is orderly, sequential, and gradual. It happens little by little, inch by inch.

Children do not always understand that human growth occurs one step at a time. They become impatient to write before their fingers can perform the task. They tackle a huge project and become frustrated by the enormity of it. They rush to complete an assignment, only to find the finished product doesn't meet their internal standard of perfection. They watch another child manipulate the computer and conclude that they will never match that skill level. These children need parents who understand human development. They need parents who realize that children are exactly where they're supposed to be and that, with support and encouragement, the next steps will occur naturally.

A reassuring hand on the shoulder and a gentle reminder, *"Inch by inch, Chad,"* can help a child relax and accept his current ability level. *"One step at a time, Ricky"* can precede teaching the notion that large goals can be broken up into smaller ones. A warm smile and *"Little by little, Caitlin"* may reduce frustration.

"Inch by inch" and similar phrases tend to reduce children's stress and give them permission to enjoy learning. This style of parent talk slows the rush to completion that dominates our product-centered society and puts more emphasis on the learning process. "Inch by inch" allows children to enjoy the process of creating a project. It helps them see that the creativity involved in planning and executing a clay pot is as valuable as the completed pottery.

"Inch by inch" encourages children to experiment, manipulate, and take risks. Parent talk of this nature invites them to relax, have fun, and become comfortable with their learning. They can get playful with tasks and take the time to talk about them. When children understand that learning takes place one step at a time and that they are developing steadily in their own unique way, they enjoy the process of learning, delighting in each small step along the way, inch by inch.

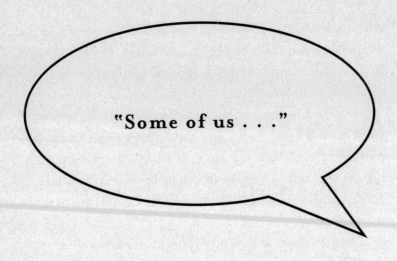

"*Some of us* play musical instruments."
"*Some of us* are into sports."
"*Some of us* drive slowly."
"*Some of us* litter."
"*Some of us* go to church regularly."

When we see children using physical intimidation, wasting resources, or calling each other names, we may be tempted to criticize or categorize in ways which separate us from them and elevate us to a superior position.

"*Some of us* . . ." reminds adults of our connectedness to our children and of our common humanity. It is inclusive language that prevents us from creating a "me vs. them" atmosphere in our homes. It communicates to children that each of us is an important individual part of a greater whole. It moves children away from I/me/my thinking toward the holistic view of us/we/our.

When we use the parent talk *"some of us,"* our language helps us connect with others by focusing attention on our commonalities. We help our children create attitudes of unity in which we sense the whole or see our part in it. We are able to live and work together harmoniously as we leave behind a "me vs. them" consciousness and expand our vision to a connected view of the world.

"I'm sorry."

No one is perfect and no one does perfect parenting. Fatigue and stress take their toll on even the most skilled parent. Yes, we all sometimes engage in behaviors and use parent talk that we wish we hadn't. At these times, an apology is in order.

If you overreact, snap at your child, or exhibit any behavior you wish you could take back, the sooner you apologize the better. Don't allow the hurtful feelings and resentment to fester in your child's heart. Use the words *"I'm sorry"* as quickly and as sincerely as possible.

Some parents worry that saying they're sorry and admitting they made a mistake will diminish their authority. Authentic authority flows from respect, and sincere apologies foster the connectedness and trust that is necessary for it to lovingly evolve.

An apology is courtesy in action, and children deserve the

same degree of courtesy that adults do. Model courtesy for them by treating them the same way you would treat a neighbor or friend. Let them see and hear how a mature adult behaves in situations where mistakes have occurred.

If you said something you regret, apologize and use your parent talk skills to explain what you really meant or communicate what you wish you had said.

> "*I'm sorry,* Kevin. I was angry and I let my temper get in the way. I don't really feel that way. I love you and I wish I hadn't used those words. What I'd like to have said is, 'I feel frustrated when I find empty milk cartons in the refrigerator and I wish you'd put them in the trash next time.'"

We all blurt out words we wish we could take back. We all behave in ways we have second thoughts about later. An occasional parental lapse won't do permanent damage, especially if it's followed with an explanation and the words *"I'm sorry."*

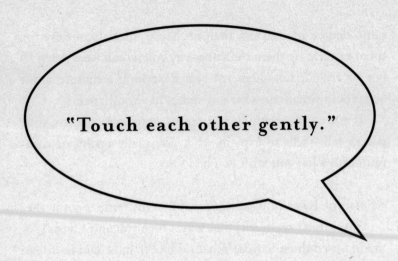

"Touch each other gently."

Some researchers believe that a minimum of eight hugs each day is necessary to maintain mental health. Others posit that if people would learn to touch one another appropriately, conflict among people and nations would be greatly reduced. The fact that elderly people and newborns can die from lack of physical touch is well documented.

Our society is currently suffering from a debilitating condition called "skin hunger." We don't get enough touch. This situation undermines our physical well-being, our mental health, and our happiness. If we wish to raise happy, healthy children, it is crucial that we teach them to touch one another in supportive and appropriate ways. To that end, we must model gentle, nurturing touching, provide a supportive environment, and encourage touch with parent talk phrases such as *"Touch each other gently."*

Children of all ages touch and manipulate their environment in order to grow. They touch to bond and connect with each other. Encouraging children to "touch each other gently" is encouraging them to learn and grow. It communicates to them that appropriate touching is accepted and valued in your home.

"Touch each other gently" is an inviting alternative to the admonition "Keep your hands to yourself." It communicates what you really mean and plants the positive picture of what you actually desire in children's minds.

When your four-year-old pushes her little sister, remind her, *"Touch each other gently."* When your third grader is poking his best friend, advise, *"Touch each other gently."* When your teenager communicates "I like you" by placing an *X* on his buddy's shoulder and preparing to slug him, insist, *"Touch each other gently."*

Sadly, many children are not skillful at soliciting the kind of touch they want and need. They satisfy their skin hunger with pokes and swats at peers and siblings, necking and petting with teenage loves, and even preadolescent sex. Their knowledge of touching has come from violent and sexually oriented television and movies, from spankings, and from societal prejudice against people touching people. So to keep them from touching, we say, "Keep your hands to yourself."

Please begin at once to teach your children that touching is important and acceptable. Teach them by modeling appropriate touch, by creating opportunities for them to come into close contact with one another, and by implementing the parent talk phrase *"Please touch each other gently."*

The Ten Best Things You Can Say
to Your Children

1. "I love you."
2. "You choose."
3. "Check it out inside."
4. "You can do anything you make up your mind to do."
5. "You always have more choices than you think you have."
6. "Every problem has a solution."
7. "What do you attribute that to?"
8. "I know you can handle it."
9. "I appreciate your efforts. Thanks."
10. "No."

Twenty Ways to Say "I Love You"
to Your Children

1. "I love you."
2. "I love you."
3. "I love you."
4. "I love you."
5. "I love you."
6. "I love you."
7. "I love you."
8. "I love you."
9. "I love you."
10. "I love you."
11. "I love you."
12. "I love you."
13. "I love you."
14. "I love you."
15. "I love you."
16. "I love you."
17. "I love you, Marti."
18. "I love you, Randy."
19. "Jenny, I love you."
20. "Matt, I love you."

Feelings

Seven Things to Say to Help Your Child
Feel Heard

1. *"Let me put this down so I can give you my full attention."*
   To help a child feel heard, we must attend with our bodies and our minds. Turn and face them. Make strong eye contact. Listen with your entire body, not just with your ears.

2. *"Wait a second while I turn off the television. I really want to hear this."*
   Eliminate distractions that could get in the way of your conversation. Turning off the TV, computer, or radio sends a silent message to the child that "You're more important than the television."

3. *"So what you mean is _____ ."*
   Frequently paraphrase as your child speaks. Paraphrasing is saying back to the other person what they just said, using your words instead of theirs. This parent talk technique demonstrates listening and proves to the child you heard him. If your paraphrase is not totally accurate, this gives him an opportunity to correct the misconception and move on with mutual understanding.

4. *"You feel _____ about _____ ."*
   Paraphrase feelings and content to show that you are listening.

5. *"Say some more about that."*

This is an invitation for the child to keep talking. It's a way of telling her it's still her turn. It lets her know that you're content to listen. It helps her feel heard and appreciated.

6. *"In other words, _____."*

This is another useful sentence starter with which you can preface a paraphrase.

7. *"Let me see if I've got this right so far."*

Use this parent talk phrase to position a paraphrase that summarizes what the child has said to this point. Again, it demonstrates listening.

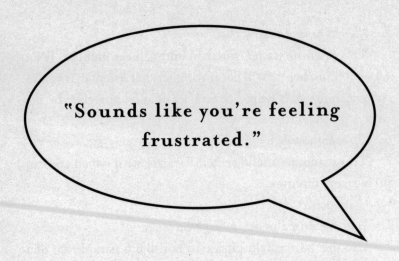

"Sounds like you're feeling frustrated."

Young children often reveal a limited vocabulary when they attempt to verbalize their feelings. Ask a youngster how she's feeling and you're likely to hear "Okay," "good," or "bad." This three-word preference for describing feelings can be attributed to two factors. First, children are not always in touch with their feelings. Second, when they are aware of their feelings, they don't have the necessary variety of words in their vocabulary to accurately describe those feelings.

Parents intent on helping their children recognize, name, and talk about feelings can utilize several parent talk strategies. Begin by talking openly about your own feelings. When you do so, use a variety of feeling words to help build your children's vocabulary.

"I'm feeling *apprehensive* about the Bears game this afternoon."

"*Frustration* is what I'm feeling right now."
"I'm *thrilled* and *ecstatic* about their decision."

Although children won't always know the meanings of the new words you're using, they'll begin to understand them as the words are used repeatedly in context. After they've heard *ecstatic* or *apprehensive* several times, they'll not only know what those words mean but they'll begin using them accurately in their own speech.

Another parent talk strategy you can use to help your children recognize and express feelings is to act as a mirror and reflect their feelings back to them. When children are expressing anger, we can mirror that expression by saying "Sounds like you're *furious* with her," or "I can see the *aggravation* on your face." When sadness appears to be their predominant feeling, we can suggest "You seem *dejected* today," or "Looks like a *glum* cloud hanging over your head."

Unless it has been modeled for them consistently, children won't often tell us how they're feeling. They need us to help them recognize and articulate those feelings as well as to understand that communicating feelings is worthwhile.

Expressing your own feelings accurately and mirroring the feelings of your children are two ways you can help them appreciate the value of sharing feelings. To do that and expand your child's feeling vocabulary at the same time, consider adding some of the following words to your parent talk.

Angry
mad
furious
irritated
aggravated
annoyed
riled up
distressed
indignant
perturbed

Upset
frustrated
bothered
depressed
troubled
distressed
perplexed

Anxious
scared
frightened
afraid
worried
nervous
unsure
apprehensive
jumpy
panicky

Sad
unhappy
depressed
miserable
dejected
lost
glum
blue
deflated
gloomy

Helpless
frustrated
powerless
confused
lost
vulnerable
deficient
ineffective
fragile
deflated

Happy
excited
delighted
cheerful
thrilled
ecstatic
proud
satisfied
thankful
content
exuberant
elated

Confident
capable
positive
determined
strong
secure
self-assured
able
full of spirit

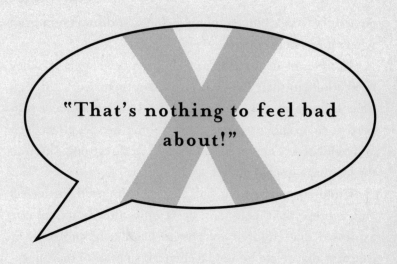

"That's nothing to feel bad about!"

"You're being way too sensitive about this."
"Come on, a hot bath will help you feel better."
"Boys [girls] your age don't cry."
"She feels bad that she did it and she's sorry."
"If you don't stop it, I'll give you something to feel
bad about."
"Other kids have it a lot worse than this."
"Put a smile on your face. Come on, get over it."
"It takes more muscles to frown than it does
to smile."
"You're overreacting. It's not that bad."
"We'll get you another goldfish to replace Molly."

A child caught up in strong emotion is in no condition to listen. This is not an appropriate time to lecture, reprimand, give

advice, try to talk him out of his feelings, or distract him from what's going on inside.

In times of strong emotion, children need support. They need adults in their lives who will help them work through their feelings in safe ways. They need an emotionally supportive environment where their feelings are acknowledged and validated. They need parent talk in direct opposition to the language quoted above.

Children need parent talk that encourages them to feel and express their emotions. It is only after emotions are expressed that children are able to handle the problems or concerns that relate to those feelings. It's not until their negative feelings come out that there is room inside for positive feelings to enter.

To help your emotion-charged child, use words that identify the feeling he is acting out. *"You sound furious"* or *"I hear how angry you are at Phillip"* acknowledge that you recognize the child's feelings. *"You seem irritated,"* or *"You really got annoyed with that teacher"* demonstrate that you are listening on a feeling level. *"That hurt, didn't it?"* or *"You sound deflated"* communicate that feelings are valued in this family and will be listened to.

Using parent talk to cheer children up, talk them out of their feelings, or distract them is ineffective. It tells them that feelings are not good, that their feelings are wrong, and that the expectation in this home is that feelings should be stuffed, hidden, and left unexpressed.

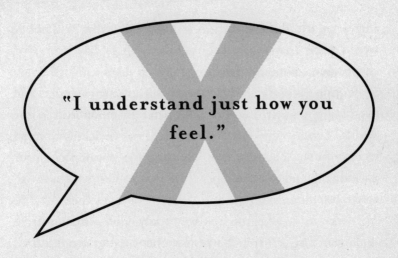

"I understand just how you feel."

"I understand just how you feel" is parent talk that attempts to empathize with our children. Parents use it to reassure children that they, too, have experienced fear, doubt, anger, or frustration. They want to communicate, "I know what that's like for you. I've been there, too. I understand."

Nobody can understand exactly how another person feels. No two people, their experiences, or their perceptions of those experiences are ever the same. We are all different and so is each of our experiences of life.

When children are experiencing strong emotion, a part of them wants to believe that no one else has ever felt that way. They want to believe that nobody has ever been this much in love or felt pain so excruciating. They want to be taken seriously for the uniqueness of their experience.

On the other hand, children want to know that their feelings are normal. They want reassurance that they will not be overwhelmed by their feelings, that others have survived those same emotions.

Because of this paradox (nobody has ever felt this way and everybody has felt this way), the parent is never sure if the words "I understand just how you feel" will be met with relief or resentment. I suggest that you drop this phrase from your parent talk, and instead *demonstrate* that you understand with active listening.

Active listening is the best way I know of to demonstrate understanding when a child is experiencing strong emotion. In order to perform this skill effectively, you must first *be quiet and listen*. Attend with your body. Give the child strong eye contact and open body posture. Get down on his level, physically. Do not interrupt his narrative. When the child stops talking, paraphrase what you heard and saw. State the feeling and a possible reason:

"You feel _____ because _____."

If Robert tells you he's mad because girls have been chasing and teasing him after school, *do not presume* you understand. Use a reflective response to check out the accuracy of your understanding. Do not use Robert's exact words. Demonstrate your understanding by paraphrasing what he said. Say "You sound angry because girls are getting after you," or "The girls are razzing you and you're upset."

If your words accurately reflect Robert's feelings, he will acknowledge that and feel understood. He is likely to continue his dialogue, blowing off steam and giving you more information. Again, use active listening skills by altering his words as you reflect back his feelings and concerns. *Remember, you are listening. This is not a time to give advice or soothe feelings. Just listen actively.*

If your initial paraphrase is inaccurate, Robert can correct the misconception by restating or embellishing his original comments. Either way, you arrive at understanding.

When Teresa shares her reaction to being cut from the softball team, refrain from saying "I know what that's like," even though you have vivid memories of being dropped from the junior varsity basketball squad. Instead, reflect her feelings and concerns in your own words. "You feel cheated because you didn't get a chance to really show your skill." It is unnecessary to give advice by telling her she shouldn't feel bad, or to help her solve her problems. All you need to do is listen skillfully. Teresa is comforted and encouraged, simply because she feels understood.

Reflective listening is an act of respect. It informs children, "I don't know exactly how you feel, but I'm ready to listen and I want to understand. I'm willing to check it out and see if I got it right. You are worth this time and energy." With practice, your active listening skills will improve. You'll notice how much your children appreciate your efforts, how they're comforted when they believe their parent really does understand their feelings and concerns. The parent-child relationship and the feelings of connectedness will grow, as will the number of times your child comes to you for listening. Your satisfaction will increase as you improve your ability to reassure your child with active listening.

> **"You can show me how you're feeling with this pillow."**

Hostile feelings need to be expressed. Since angry acts toward others or their property are not permitted in loving families, angry feelings can be channeled into symbolic or creative behaviors. To do this, use parent talk that allows angry feelings and at the same time limits angry acts.

"Your sister is not for punching. *Show me* with this doll how you're feeling."

"You seem really furious with your father. How about *writing* that in your journal?"

"It must hurt not being invited to the party. *Draw me* a picture of how you're feeling right this minute."

Hurtful *actions* need to be stopped immediately. Hurtful *feelings* need to be expressed and redirected into appropriate behaviors.

> "Trucks are not for throwing. Stomp your feet and yell as loud as you want to *show me* your anger."
> "Here, use this pillow. *Pretend* it's your brother. Hitting your brother is not allowed. Hitting this pillow is okay."

This style of parent talk communicates to children that there is a difference between wanting to hit someone and hitting someone, that desires don't always need to be acted out. There is a difference between feelings and behaviors, and one does not have to follow the other.

"Don't you talk to me like that!"

Children often challenge adults with comments such as, "I don't have to," "You can't make me," or "What makes you think you're so smart?" They use their words as bait in an attempt to distract our attention from the real issue and hook us into a power struggle.

If you hear yourself respond with "Don't you talk to me like that!" be assured you have swallowed the hook. You're caught, and the struggle is on.

"Don't you talk to me like that!" is parent talk that indicates you have interpreted the child's words as attack. Perceiving attack, you become defensive. Defensiveness prevents you from accurately hearing the real content of the child's message. As you defend yourself, the conflict escalates.

It is possible to respond effectively to antagonistic statements by remembering that angry children feel attacked and afraid. Their words are unskillful cries for help. I suggest that you focus on the feelings of the child involved. Temporarily ignore the verbal content of his message and speak to his feelings rather than to his words. *"You must be furious to talk like that. Let's talk about it when you're less upset"* responds to the youngster's feelings and lets him know you're taking him seriously. *"I hear your anger and I'd like you to express it in different words"* acknowledges the strong emotion. It tells the child that you dislike his choice of words, but you care about his pain. *"You're really upset. It's not like you to talk like that"* shifts the emphasis from *what* your son said to the emotion behind it.

Recently I witnessed a secondary science teacher initiate a discussion about tardiness with one late student. "Oh, lighten up!" the student replied with a roll of her eyes. This teacher responded with skill and understanding. He analyzed the outburst as an attempt to divert attention from the real problem. *"Becky, I sense your frustration and can see your tardiness is not as big a concern to you as it is to me. I want to discuss it further. Meet me after class,"* he told her. Comfortable in his teaching stance, he ignored further grumbling by the student and continued with his lesson.

This teacher responded to the student's feelings with professionalism instead of emotionalism. He refused to speak from a defensive or counterattacking position and did not get "hooked." He was not distracted by the student's unskillful, even hostile, way of expressing herself and was able to empower her while retaining his own sense of personal power. Later, when the student calmed down, he would deal specifically with the issue of tardiness.

Centering your response on children's feelings rather than on their rebellious choice of words helps you to acknowledge their feelings without reacting defensively. It lets them know you heard them at a deeper level. It keeps you in control and keeps their dignity intact.

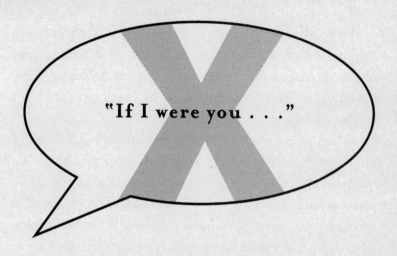

"If I were you . . ."

"If I were you, I'd choose the first book."
"If I were you, I'd ignore him and walk away."
"If I were you, I'd change my attitude."

Notice that advice follows statements that begin *"If I were you."* When you give advice, only two things can happen. A child can take it or leave it. If he leaves it by ignoring or rejecting the advice, you grow resentful. ("I gave him a great idea, and he failed to implement it; I'll be darned if I'll give him any more advice.") If the child takes your advice and dislikes the results, *he* grows resentful. You lose stature in his eyes.

Some children actually seek advice to prove that the advice is worthless. They make sure it doesn't work. It's a way for them to feel superior by proving the parent wrong. It's their way of gaining a greater sense of personal power.

If the advice turns out to be "helpful," children will return to you for more advice in the future. As their faith in your advice increases, their belief in themselves decreases. They learn to turn away from themselves and seek solutions from others. Their personal power fades.

When we offer instant advice, we deprive our children of the experience of wrestling with their own problems. We eliminate time for them to think, to struggle, and to make personal decisions. Often they resent our quick solution to what they perceive as a complex problem. When we quickly solve dilemmas that children perceive to be difficult, they're likely to feel inferior and unempowered.

Most advice is unsolicited. For example, when my son Matt graduated from elementary school, his sixth-grade teacher told him that he could invite two guests to the graduation ceremony and party. I was scheduled to work out of town that day and couldn't attend. Matt's mother appreciated and accepted the invitation, as did Matt's nineteen-year-old sister, Jenny. A few days later, however, Jenny announced that she intended to bring her boyfriend Don.

Matt now had a problem and was unsure how to solve it. Should he withdraw the invitation to his sister? Should he tell her not to bring her boyfriend? Maybe he should just avoid the issue and show up at the graduation party with too many guests. He took his dilemma to the teacher. Her response was immediate: "You'll have to tell your sister not to bring her boyfriend."

Later that night, Matt followed his teacher's advice. He called his sister at college and told her the bad news. His words were predicable, considering the way the situation was handled. "*My teacher said* Don can't come," he told his sister. His language revealed that he did not own the problem *or* the solution.

This young man was about to enter junior high school. His teacher prepared him poorly for that experience by taking away his opportunity to consider conflicting issues, grapple with inconsistencies, and solve problems on his own. He learned that "Adults know best. Kids can't trust their own judgment. Somebody else will think for me and will do it better."

Adults who empower children do not give unsolicited advice. They see their job as that of helping the child generate solutions, sort through thoughts and feelings, and gain confidence through decision making and problem solving. They understand that it is important for children to make some mistakes in judgment. Learning comes from experiencing the positive *and* the negative consequences of decisions. I suggest the following guidelines:

1. *Postpone instant advice. Listen.*

2. *Encourage youngsters to keep talking. Say, "Tell me more" or "Keep going," parent talk phrases that invite the child to expand on what he sees as the problem and possible solutions.*

3. *Restate the problem as a question. "You're not sure which book to choose for your report?" "You're unclear what to do when he calls you names?"*

4. *Use wait time when you restate the problem as a question. Be silent. Give children time to think. Solutions usually follow.*

Clearly, parents have a right and an obligation to share their experiences and ideas with their youngsters. We possess adult wisdom, and it is important that we share it in helpful ways. *Ask* if the child would like help generating ideas. If he answers yes, preface your suggestions with parent talk sentence starters that help the child retain responsibility.

"How would you feel about . . . ?"
"Would you consider . . . ?"
"How would you like . . . ?"

These sentence starters acknowledge that your suggestion may not be the child's best answer. They make it clear that the child is responsible for choosing and implementing a solution. They leave the decision-making process where it belongs, in the heart and in the mind of the child.

"Say you're sorry."

John hit his little brother with a truck. His dad made him say he was sorry.
Jenny forgot to send her grandmother a birthday card. Her parents made her call and say she was sorry.
Sarah got so upset at her mother, she swore at her. Her father made her say she was sorry.

"Tell him you're sorry" is parent talk that is used with good intentions. It does not usually produce good results. Our words are "Tell him you're sorry." But the real message we send our children when we choose those words is "Forget what you'd really like to say. Hold back your anger. Choke off your frustration. Push down all your real feelings and pretend they don't exist."

Whenever we ask angry children to apologize, we do

them a disservice by teaching them to deny their feelings. It's unhealthy for children to believe that some feelings are better than others, that "negative" feelings should not be expressed or felt, and that pretending is more important than expressing authentic feelings. Instead, we must allow them to experience their feelings and express them in responsible ways that lead to the resolution of problems and to more comfortable feelings.

Sometimes *"Tell him you're sorry"* gives children an easy out. It's a simple penance that excuses them from considering a change in their behavior. They don't have to create plans for more appropriate action or think about how to behave differently in the future. They don't have to think at all. They only have to say "I'm sorry."

If a child is not sorry, don't coerce her into pretending differently. Use your skills to help her get in touch with her real feelings and communicate them in descriptive, nonjudgmental language. Say *"Tell him you're angry because when he called you stupid it felt like a put-down,"* or *"Let Bob know you're frustrated at the amount of time he's taking with the computer game."*

If a child *is* sorry, certainly she can be encouraged to say so. This can be a cleansing release that allows the child to get on with her day. When real regret exists, help children learn from their mistakes. Teach your children to express what they've learned from their behavior and what they're going to do differently next time. This is enough. Children do *not* have to feel remorse, regret, or self-criticism to learn from mistakes.

"I learned that you don't like me talking to you while you're on the telephone, and it's my intention to wait until you're finished

next time," and *"I learned you don't like me eating all the pie, and I intend to save you a couple of pieces next time"* leave the child feeling more powerful and self-responsible than "I'm sorry I did it. I apologize. Please forgive me."

"I'm sorry" language leaves the child focusing on wrong-doing, feeling small, and hoping to be forgiven. It's a way of speaking that lowers self-esteem, personal power, and confidence. The goal-directed "I learned and I intend" style helps her focus on learning and positive intention.

It's less important to say we're sorry than to behave as if it is so. When we drop the *"Tell him you're sorry"* phrase from our parent talk, we help our children concentrate on learning. We teach them the valuable lesson that to be sorry means to behave differently.

"REMEMBER THE GOOD OLD DAYS WHEN ALL WE HAD TO DO TO GET OUT OF SOMETHING WAS TO SAY WE WERE SORRY?"

Increasing
Conflict

Ten Things to Say to Increase Conflict

1. "You're lying."
2. "This is my house. You'll do it my way."
3. "You don't know what you're talking about."
4. "If you don't like it, tough."
5. "What I say, goes."
6. "I'm not interested in what you think."
7. "Tell it to somebody who cares."
8. "You're not old enough to understand."
9. "When I tell you to do something, you jump."
10. "Because I'm right, that's why."

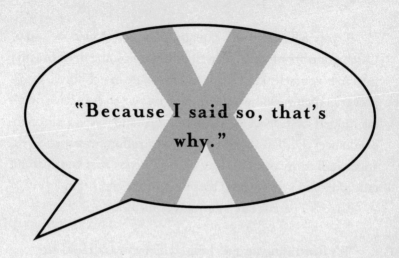

"Because I said so, that's why."

The words that fill the air are *"Because I said so. That's why!"* But the message accompanying these words is: I'm big and you're little. I'm smart and you're dumb. I have power and you don't. My job is to tell; your job is to obey. I don't have to listen to you, but you'd better listen to me. I don't take suggestions, I give them. You can't possibly figure this out, so you need me to tell you what to do.

Sometimes "because-I-said-so" parent talk originates from a power-hungry adult intent on maintaining control. Other times it comes from a frustrated parent tired of answering a child's seemingly endless list of questions. On occasion it can be a sign that a loving parent has temporarily run out of patience with a child who wants to argue. Whatever the motivation, *"Because I said so"* lacks respect and needs to be eliminated from your parent talk repertoire.

If you hear yourself explain, *"Because I said so,"* stop. Catch your breath and call a time-out. Do some deep breathing. Ask yourself: Do I want to empower my children, or *do* power *to* them? Do I want to model respect so they have mental models of respect in action, or demand respect through obedience? Do I want to express frustration, impatience, or anger in healthy or unhealthy ways? Reconstruct your parent talk after you've answered these questions and begin again.

Effective parent talk alternatives include:

"It's frustrating for me, John, when you ask rapid-fire questions. Here's the answer to the last one. And please give me a fifteen-minute rest before you ask the next one."
"I'll give you a reason if your desire is simply to understand it. If you want a reason so you can argue about it, I won't give you one. You decide."
"Mary, I'm the parent here. You're the child. It's my job as the parent to make some of the decisions I feel are important. This is one of those times when I'm deciding for you."
"Rebecca, whining and arguing don't work with me. If you want me to listen, tell me in a normal voice."

Imagine your personal response if I answered, "Because I said so, that's why!" to your question about why you should read this book. Your internal dialogue might be, "Who does he think he is?" or "Nobody can tell me what to do!"

"Because I said so" invites resistance and resentment. It builds walls between people and creates distance. It works against our parenting goals of building connectedness and unity in our families.

Hear "Because I said so" as a signal that you're allowing power, impatience, or frustration to take over your communication style. Use this red-flag phrase to awaken yourself and move to a gentler, more loving way of communicating, not because I said so, but because both you and your children are worth it.

"WHAT KIND OF PARENT TALK COULD I HAVE USED? THEY _ARE_ HER MOST EASTERY SHOES."

"Okay, who did it?"

Parents often ask, "Who did it?" in order to gain information. We want to know who ate the cookies. Who broke the window? Who left peanut butter and jelly on the counter? If the question is answered correctly, we obtain the name of an offender.

Yet the question "Who did it?" often gives more information than it gets. It communicates to the child that the parent cares about finding fault and fixing blame. It points to the parent as someone who cares more about punishment than about the search for solutions.

"Who did it?" is beside the point. It draws attention to *who* is the problem rather than *what* is the problem. It creates a loser and brands someone as wrong. It serves to keep the point focused on blame instead of on seeking solutions.

"Who left the paintbrushes in the sink?" doesn't give children information about the parent's feelings. It doesn't focus on what needs to be done *now*. It gives the child no clues as to what behaviors the parent expects in the future. It is not a teaching tool but a prelude to punishment.

One variation, "Okay, whose fault was it?" is especially unhelpful. Two preschool children in one family recently answered this question by pointing to each other. This style of parent talk encourages children to live out a "me vs. them" attitude. It invites them to engage in self-preservation at the expense of others.

As an alternative, I suggest that parents describe the situation and state their feelings. "I see paintbrushes in the sink, and I'm angry." "I notice paint on the carpet, and I'm irritated." It's also useful in these situations to give children information. "The paint just spilled. We need a sponge." "When paint gets spilled, it stains."

When parents share their feelings, describe the situation, and provide information, they send a different message. The message is that they believe children are intelligent enough to choose an appropriate action once they have the necessary information.

Next time you hear yourself say, "Who did it?"—stop. Question your own motives. What is more important—identifying the culprit or focusing on what needs to be done? Let your parent talk reflect your answer.

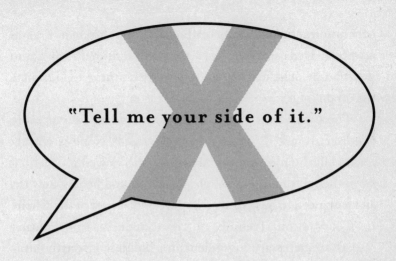

"Tell me your side of it."

Sides exist in competitive games, courtrooms, and war. They have no place in families where connectedness, belonging, and oneness are encouraged. *Side* is the key word here. If there is one side, there must be another. This hints that someone is right and someone is wrong and serves to solidify adversarial relationships. "Tell me your side of it" pits one child against another. It promotes a "me vs. you" mindset that encourages people to put distance between one another and their positions. It communicates separateness and invites polarization.

An alternative to "Tell me your side of it" is to ask children to share their perception or help you appreciate their thinking. You might ask, "How did you see that?" or "How does it seem to you?"

When we ask children to communicate their thinking, they will describe many thought processes, rationales, and conclusions. When those differences are listened to and acknowledged, children learn that different ideas can stand side by side. The existence of one does not have to eliminate the other.

There will be a variety of responses when two or more children are asked *"How did you see that?"* None is wrong. Each child is an expert on how he or she viewed a situation. Even though their perceptions, thoughts, and beliefs conflict, all views need to be respected and treated as part of the whole.

Cooperation, feelings of connectedness, and mutual respect are necessary ingredients for building effective families. These concepts can be promoted in your family by choosing parent talk that helps youngsters see that, in reality, we are all on the same side *together*.

"Did you win?"

After Kathryn's track meet, Elizabeth's softball game, and Robert's defense of first-chair trumpet, each child's mother asked, "Did you win?"

Kathryn came in last in the hundred-yard dash.
Elizabeth's team lost the game by one run.
Robert successfully defended his band position.

Because each parent directed her interest toward winning, she missed an opportunity to help her child focus on the many joys and satisfactions of competition. According to traditional thought, only one of these children won: Robert. In our society, there is a pervasive belief that each event, competition, or category can applaud only one winner. In fact, there is a cultural obsession with being first, so it is crucial for parents to seize opportunities to help their children focus on events instead of outcomes and to move attention to the pleasures of participating.

The obsession to be first separates. It creates unrealistic expectations and places unreasonable demands on competitors. During the Winter Olympics I watched a young man agonize because he had lost the downhill ski competition. The announcer referred to him as a "loser." In fact, he had missed skiing the fastest downhill run *ever* by two-hundredths of a second. *Hundredths* of a second! A loser?

I know an eighth grader who refused to go out for track because people might ridicule him for running too slowly. "But *you* are out there running," I argued. "*They* are just sitting there! You deserve admiration no matter what your time or place." He shook his head. "But I won't win." He chose to give up an opportunity to be with his friends, have fun, and gain attention from his peers because he was afraid to lose.

I used to run ten-kilometer road races. My five-year-old didn't understand that I "won" whether I finished first or four hundredth. I know I win if I have fun, meet new friends, enjoy a sunny day or a warm rain. I win when I finish the race and feel the support of cheering spectators. I win when I achieve my timing goal or set a new record for myself. I win improved health and self-esteem that flows from the self-discipline and commitment of daily runs. No matter how I explain, the five-year-old does not understand. Already, he has caught "must-win fever." I tell him, "Yes, I won. And I wasn't first."

In order to be happy and successful, children must learn to deal effectively with competition. They must learn to accept "wins" *and* "losses" with the grace that comes from understanding that "wins" are only part of the pleasure of competition. Camaraderie, testing oneself, belonging, effort, and learning are all important parts of the competitive process. Winning does not necessarily mean being "first." We can begin to communicate this to our children by changing our parent talk to *"What did you like about it?"*

"What did you like about it?" asks children to consider various aspects of the competition. It asks that they focus on the pleasurable ones. People tend to notice what they don't like about an activity. It's important that they notice what they *do* like. Youngsters develop thinking skills as they reconstruct the competition in their minds, analyzing and evaluating.

Relationships develop and expand because *"What did you like about it?"* requires more than a one-word response. Dialogue is encouraged as children elaborate on activities and converse with the parent about interests.

I believe that many children miss countless opportunities to develop talents, learn, and have fun because they're afraid they won't win. Kathryn was a winner because she *ran* the hundred-yard dash. Elizabeth won because she has developed her skills to a level where she has been asked to join a traditionally all-male baseball team. Robert is a winner, too, not because he beat the opposition but because he had never played as well as he did while defending his first chair, and he knows it. All children are capable of winning and feeling like winners if society's obsession with being "first" does not rob them of experiencing themselves as winners.

Parents can help their children move beyond this limited and limiting view of competition by changing "Did you win?" to *"What did you like about it?"*

"Why did you do that?"

Well-intentioned parents who desire information to solve problems, often ask, "Why did you do that?" However, it may also be asked by adults wanting to fix blame and deliver criticism. To avoid its negative use, consider the issue of timing when you're tempted to use this question as part of your parent talk.

Children have learned from experience that "why" is often a prelude to criticism. When they hear it immediately following a specific behavior, they don't hear, "Why did you do that?" They hear, "Why did you ever do something so ridiculous, so stupid?" They hear it as an attack. When they perceive the question as an attack, they experience anxiety and defensiveness, which do not lead to clear or rational thinking about behavior.

"Why did you do that?" is often a demand, an accusation

directed at children that takes the focus off the behavior and creates a power struggle between parent and child. Many times children simply don't know why they did something. When they don't know, they're not able to accurately articulate why they chose to hit or spit or get angry. Even if they have the capability to figure out *why,* they're probably too afraid or anxious to give us an answer.

There are times when "Why did you do that?" *is* productive. Brought up later in the day, it can generate information useful in the search for solutions. Since some time has elapsed between the behavior and the question, there is less chance that it will be heard as an attack.

The next time you hear yourself use the phrase *"Why did you do that?"* notice the delivery. Is it a question or an accusation? Is it a search for solutions or a device intended to fix blame? Is it used to help children or to get after them? Does it really matter "why"?

If it doesn't matter why a child chose a certain behavior, don't ask about it. If it does seem important, ask later, when the tension and emotion have dissipated.

"What did I tell you?"
"See. I knew it."
"You didn't believe me, did you? Now you know."
"I guess that proves I was right."
"That's what I said, remember?"

Being right feels good. It's a way of proving our worth to ourselves. It helps us to be on top, to reaffirm our own intelligence, to claim superiority. Being right is vindication with proof. There's only one problem: *Being right doesn't work.*

Being right breeds resentment. Any time you make yourself right about something, you make someone else wrong. Children as well as adults don't enjoy being in the role of being wrong. Saying "I told you so" to a child rubs his nose in the fact that he was incorrect. It's hard enough for children to accept being wrong without adding increased pressure. Reminding them that you were right only makes it more difficult for them to admit to themselves that they were wrong.

I'm reminded of a cartoon that showed a patient in a hospital bed bandaged from head to toe, with both legs and arms in traction. The doctor stood near the bed looking at her clipboard as the patient explained, "But I had the right of way."

Did being right prevent the accident? No. Did being right eliminate pain and suffering? No. Did being right work in this case? Absolutely not! And being right won't work with your children either.

You can be right about the capital of Nevada if you want to. You can be right about the teacher's reaction to the late paper. You can be right about the cost of the gym shoes, the amount of gas it takes to fill the tank, or the number of days it took the fish to die in the fish tank. As a parent, you'll have an infinite number of opportunities to be right. And you'll have an equal number of chances to say, "I told you so," and remind the entire family who it was that was right. You *can* be right. But at whose expense and at what price?

Is it worth being right about the capital of Nevada if you create distance between you and your son? Is it worth being right about the number of days it took the fish to die if it makes your daughter wrong? Is it worth saying, "I told you so," when resentment builds and connectedness dissolves in your family?

Most of the time, children realize they were wrong and don't need to be told. When you're right, gloat privately. Refrain from using parent talk that announces your rightness. You and I will both benefit. You'll be glad you did, and I won't have to say "I told you so."

Reducing
Conflict

Ten Things to Say to Reduce Conflict

1. "Let's both take a ten-minute time-out."
2. "How can we both get what we want?"
3. "Let's search for a solution together on this one."
4. "I'm willing to compromise. Are you?"
5. "Let's negotiate."
6. "What's your opinion?"
7. "Help me to understand your point of view."
8. "How can we see this a different way?"
9. "It feels like we're working against each other on this. Let's both remember we're on the same team here."
10. "I'd like your input on this."

"I see clothes on the floor."

There is a game that is played in homes throughout the world by people of all ages and nationalities. Although any number of people can play, two works best. Usually, it pits children against parents. This game has no written rules. Since it is often played unconsciously, participants are usually unaware that they are planning strategies or executing moves. No one acknowledges that the game is on, though it can be played several times a day with intensity and feeling. It's called the *command/resistance game*.

All parents have played this game. It goes like this. Parents command; children resist. Then the process is repeated. Parents command; children resist. Many rounds can be executed in this game, usually with no winner. And the game goes on day after day. Parents command and children resist.

Children resist because resistance is a typical and normal

response to being told what to do. Both adults and children respond with resistance, reluctance, and resentment when confronted with orders and commands. Neither big people nor little people like being told what to do.

Children are willing players of the command/resistance game. They're told what to do so often by parents, teachers, and other adults that they've acquired the strategy of automatically resisting *any* directive given by an adult. They're so busy actively resisting commands, they often don't even hear the content of the message. When a parent's order is ignored, he or she may choose to get louder and more commanding in order to be taken seriously. Children respond to that ploy by digging in their heels. As the cycle continues, both adult and child are left feeling frustrated and powerless.

There is only one way to win the command/resistance game. Refuse to play. Instead of telling children what to do, use parent talk that describes the situation at hand and leaves the "what to do" part up to them. *You* state the situation as you see it, and *they* decide what to do.

An alternative to ordering children to "Quiet down" is to respond, *"I'm being distracted by the noise."* Instead of commanding "Get over here for dinner," announce *"I'm ready to start serving dinner."* Say *"Your clothes are on the floor,"* to replace the directive "Put your clothes in the hamper."

Eliminating orders and commands from your parent talk decreases defiance. It communicates to your children that you think they are intelligent enough to create appropriate responses once they understand the situation. It allows them to make the choice of how to respond. When you communicate without commands, you invite your children to use their intelligence to respond in ways that make sense to them. At the same time, you lessen the odds that they will react with resistance and perpetuate the no-win command/resistance game.

> "I don't like what I just heard. If you're angry, tell me another way."

Sometimes name-calling is directed at parents. It may take a gentle form of attack such as "You're clumsy." It could be sent wrapped in judgment like "That's stupid." Or it might even take on a sarcastic edge: "You gotta be kidding!" Whatever form it takes, skill is necessary to deal with it effectively. A skillful response I suggest is *"I don't like what I just heard. If you're angry, please tell me another way."* This phrase communicates respect for yourself and respect for the child.

When you share this key phrase with children, you're really saying "I have too much respect for myself to be talked to this way. Please share your thoughts and feelings in a way that honors me as a person." This form of communication also shows respect for the child. It announces *"I think your feelings are important. You have a right to express them here. I will listen to you and consider your feedback. Please tell me in a way that gives me useful information."*

When you use this form of parent talk with children, you're modeling self-respect in action. You're not only teaching them how *you* want to be treated, you're showing them a way to communicate how *they* wish to be treated.

"EXCELLENT COMMUNICATION SKILLS. POOR CHOICE OF WORDS."

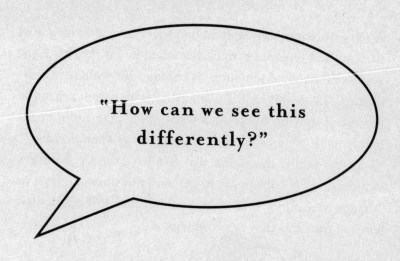

"How can we see this differently?"

When a child is agonizing over a perceived injustice, encourage him to consider another point of view by asking *"How can we see this differently?"*

When a difficult situation must be endured, help children experience peace of mind through acceptance of the inevitable by asking *"How can we see this differently?"*

When your family is indignant about a situation, encourage tolerance and defenselessness by asking *"How can we see this differently?"*

Children in conflict tend to get caught up in their own point of view. They develop tunnel vision and can see things only one way. Their beliefs become truths to them, and their perceptions become facts.

One parent was confronted by his twelve-year-old daughter who was upset with her second-semester school schedule.

A self-awareness, self-exploration program for middle school students had replaced gym on her schedule for the first eight weeks of the second semester. "It's unfair," the youngster complained. "I hate this junk. I want gym." This parent began the process of moving his child toward developing more open-mindedness when he asked, *"How can we see this differently?"*

In the family discussion that followed, family members brainstormed possible ways to perceive the situation; how to "change your mind" even if you couldn't change the situation. Some of the ideas they came up with are:

"Well, you sure will appreciate gym more when you get it."
"At least this new class is something different."
"It's probably better than math."
"You could view it as a challenge."

Children learned through this exercise in perception that it's possible to see the same thing from different angles. When children learn that opposing ideas can stand together, they've taken an important step toward effective problem solving and conflict resolution.

The parent talk phrase *"How can we see this differently?"* can remind you, the parent, of the importance of shifting perspective. One parent I know used this phrase to reduce stress during her quiet reading time. She had just begun when she heard a knock on the front door. As she opened the door, she immediately recognized that her eight-year-old had a nosebleed.

"Johnny hit me," he said.

"No, I didn't," replied the accused, who stood directly behind this parent's child.

"This is just great," the parent muttered to herself. "Now I won't get my only quiet reading period of the entire day."

She felt disgruntled, helpless, and totally victimized. Then she recognized that this was an opportunity to change her own mind *even if she couldn't change the situation.* She employed this suggested piece of parent talk by taking a deep breath and asking herself, *"How can I see this differently?"* Within seconds she answered herself. "This is an opportunity to help these children learn problem-solving skills. I'd rather do it later, but it's happening now. I can handle it."

Seeing the situation as an opportunity instead of a disaster, this parent was able to respond effectively. She put down her book, went to the two boys, and helped them define their problem. Once the problem was defined, she asked them to generate a list of solutions and pick one on which they could both agree. She told them to let her know when they had finished, and she returned to her quiet reading time. She was able to relax and enjoy her reading knowing that she had chosen to view the situation in a way that was helpful to everyone concerned.

Whenever you feel exasperated, frustrated, or without hope, ask yourself, *"How can I see this differently?"* Take a moment to relax and take a deep breath. Trust that an answer, *your* answer, will come. It will enable you to shift your perception to a less stressful, more constructive view.

"How can we see this differently?" will help both parents and children remember that even when circumstances must be endured, we *can* change our perception. We can experience these inevitable family parenting situations without stress and distress by learning to see them differently.

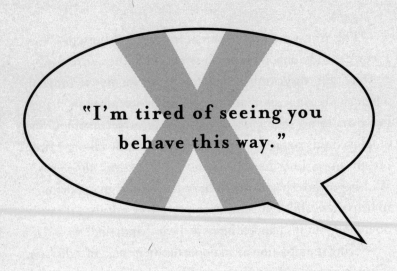

"I'm tired of seeing you behave this way."

"I don't like what I'm seeing."
"I'm seeing way too much of that!"

These phrases are intended to send the message "I don't like that behavior." When parents use them, they hope their children tune into the signal.

Yet the same phrases can be used to send a different type of signal, one that prompts the parent to engage in a round of inner exploration. When you hear yourself say "I'm tired of seeing you behave this way," stop. Spend some time reflecting on how you *would* like to see your child. Perhaps it is time to see her some other way.

Each of us sees things differently because we do not see through our eyes only. We see through the filters of our beliefs, values, ideas, attitudes, and total life experiences.

We then interpret what we see in our own unique way.

This phenomenon occurs in whatever we see. We look at an event and project onto it whatever it is we have within us. Some people see a good day, while others see a bad day. Yet, it's the same day. Some see child X as a troublemaker, others as a potential leader. And it's the same child. How we see something or someone tells more about *us* than it does about who or what we saw. It tells about our beliefs, attitudes, and values. It tells what we have been projecting outward.

Perception is a choice. How we see children is not fixed. Our perceptions are flexible and under our control. It is possible to see children as troublemakers or as crying out for help. We can perceive cheaters or see children who do not yet know that playing the game honestly has more value than winning. We can see children as mouthy or as young people struggling to get their social needs met.

Perception is critical, because how you see what goes on in your family affects how you react to it. If you choose to see kids cheating at a card game as awful, you're more likely to blame and punish. If you see cheating as an opportunity to help children learn that participating is more important than winning and losing, you're more likely to use problem-solving techniques.

"I don't like what I'm seeing" or "I'm tired of seeing you behave this way" can serve as a caution to you. It is one indication that you're choosing to see children in a negative light.

Often, we define children by their actions. We label them as troublemakers, liars, procrastinators, complainers, or reluctant learners. In order to be of help to them, we need to learn to see beyond their act to their essence.

Troublemakers are just doing their troublemaker act.

Reluctant children are doing their reluctant act. Bullies are doing their bully act. But that is not the essence of their real selves. It is not the truth about them. It is just an act. We are all much more than our act. Each of us is valuable in our own right, regardless of our act. No matter how unskilled our behavior, our intent is to solicit love and acceptance.

If *we* don't see beyond our children's acts, who will? If *we* don't communicate to them that in spite of their act *we* see their worth shining through, who will?

"I don't like what I'm seeing here" is parent talk that can serve as a signal that you have lost sight of your child's real worth. Whether you say it aloud or silently, hear it as a sign that it's time to question how you are perceiving your child. Ask yourself, *"How am I seeing this?"* If you don't like the answers and are dissatisfied with your perceptions, ask for help. Go to the quiet place within yourself. Center yourself. Touch that place where you tap your inner knowing and ask *"How else can I see this? What else could I be seeing here? How can I see this differently?"*

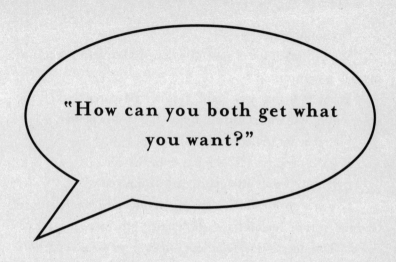

"How can you both get what you want?"

Jesse and Jamie were fourteen- and thirteen-year-old siblings. They were expected to work together to rake the front lawn. After a few minutes of work time, a heated discussion erupted.

"Why won't you ever cooperate?" Jamie accused.

"Everything always has to be your way!" Jesse slung back. A family crisis was in the making.

The father approached the boys calmly and commented, "Looks as if you have a problem."

"I want to finish this job now."

"I want to do it later."

The parent put a calming hand on each child's shoulder. "What is it that you want, Jamie?"

"I want to finish now so I can get to baseball practice this afternoon."

"Say some more."

"We promised we'd have this done today, and the rest of my day is committed."

"What is it that *you* want, Jesse?" the parent asked the other child, without commenting on the first explanation.

"I don't want to do it now."

"What *do* you want?" the father persisted.

"I want to watch my favorite television show."

"So *you* want to watch a specific show and *Jamie* wants to be done in time for his baseball practice," the parent summarized. "The question is, *How can you both get what you want?* Please talk about that and see if you can find an answer that's acceptable to both of you," he told them. "I'll check with you later." Then he turned and walked away.

A short time later, the teens approached their father. Both looked satisfied and appeared to be friendly. Jesse said, "I'm going to tape my show, and we'll rake the lawn now. I'll watch it when Jamie's at baseball practice."

The father smiled in affirmation of their solution. "Glad you worked it out," he said. Later he would engage the children in a discussion of how they were able to solve the problem together once they had redefined it.

Jesse really didn't need to rake the yard later. That was not the real problem. His true concern was being able to watch his show. The solution worked for both boys. Neither had to give up anything; both got what they wanted.

"How can you both get what you want?" is parent talk that builds interdependence and encourages cooperation. It helps children work together to redefine problems and search for acceptable solutions.

The dictionary defines cooperation as "working together toward a common end." The important words are *together* and *common.* *"How can you both get what you want?"* helps children work on a problem together to find a common solution.

Children in conflict usually focus on "winning" an encounter because experience has taught them that compromise means giving up what they want. Compromise means that everybody loses something. Even the most altruistic child is unwilling to compromise if it means always losing part of what she wants.

"How can you both get what you want?" helps children redefine problems in terms of wants and needs instead of winners and losers. It opens up options where previously there seemed to be none. It encourages cooperation, so *everyone* wins. You can help your children work together to solve problems so they can both win.

The next time your children seem deadlocked on an issue, show your confidence and support by using parent talk that asks, *"How can you both get what you want?"*

Campbell.

"WE'D BETTER QUIT THIS, OR WE'LL HAVE TO DO PROBLEM SOLVING AT THE NEXT FAMILY MEETING."

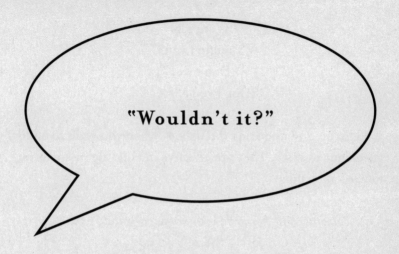

"Wouldn't it?"

Having trouble getting your child to come to agreement? Is a verbal commitment difficult for him to make? Is he slipping into indecision and staying there? Then perhaps it's time to add tie-downs to your parent talk.

Tie-downs are a way of framing your parent talk to get a positive verbal response from your child. They consist of phrases you attach to a question to increase your chances of getting an affirmative commitment. Some examples are:

"Aren't they?"
"Can't you?"
"Doesn't it?"
"Haven't they?"
"Isn't that correct?"
"Won't you?"

"Wasn't it?"
"Couldn't you?"
"Don't we?"
"Don't you agree?"

Use tie-downs during discussions when you want to build an avenue of yeses. They are effective in building momentum toward agreement.

"So you chose not to do your homework, didn't you?"
"Yes."
"That violated our agreement, didn't it?"
"Yes."
"You can guess what that means, can't you?"
"I think so."
*"A weekend night at home was our agreement for a decision
to skip homework, wasn't it?"*
"Yes, it was."
*"Then you won't be surprised when I follow through on our
agreement, will you?"*
"No."

As you learn to connect a tie-down to your questions, you'll receive more consistent yeses from your children.

"You know how your sister feels about that, *don't you?*"
"So you'll correct that situation first thing tomorrow,
won't you?"
"He was really upset by that, *wasn't he?*"
"Your coach has given you that feedback before, *hasn't he?*"

"This could get you in trouble at school, *couldn't it?*"

Tie-downs are a gentle way to lead your child toward agreement and remind her of obligations and commitments. With this style of parent talk you will have fewer arguments and experience less resistance. You will start using this technique right away, *won't you?*

"You're probably right."

"You're probably right" is parent talk that can be used to diffuse anger and keep an argument from escalating. It's a technique that focuses the child on the problem at hand and encourages him to look inward rather than away from himself for responsibility and solutions.

Brandon was a responsible sixteen-year-old who took the privilege of driving a car seriously. He passed driver's training with an A, always wore a seat belt, and drove the speed limit without exception. He honored his father's request to make sure his friends didn't smoke during those times they were in his dad's car. There was only one problem. Gas. Or the lack of it.

Brandon's father experienced three separate incidents of driving the car the morning after his son used it, only to find the gas gauge at or below empty. Although the situation didn't occur every time Brandon used the car, the frequency was enough to encourage his father to create new guidelines.

"If you choose to bring the car back with half a tank of gas or more," Brandon's father explained, "you'll be choosing to use the car again the next weekend night if we're not using it. If you choose to bring the car back with less than half a tank of gas, then you're choosing not to use the car the next weekend night. You can show me your choice by how much gas is in the car."

Fair enough, thought Brandon. Fair, that is, until he forgot about the new guidelines and returned the car one Friday night with the gas gauge hovering close to the one-quarter mark.

"Thanks for letting me know you're choosing not to use the car tonight," Brandon's father informed his son the next morning. Those words set off a torrent of excuses, explanations, and pleadings from Brandon, to each of which his father responded with the parent talk phrase *"You're probably right."*

"Come on, Dad, please. I've got to have the car tonight. It's my turn to drive. If I don't get the car, the guys will all be mad at me."

"You're probably right."

"And I promised my girlfriend I'd take her to the mall this afternoon. She's gonna be ticked off, too."

"You're probably right."

"I won't do it again, Dad. You'll see."

"Probably so."

"You're the only father in the entire city who would be this mean."

"That's probably true."

"I would have filled the car with gas, but I was going to be late. Which is more important: being home on time or having gas in the car?"

"They're both important to me. And when you choose to return the car with less than half a tank of gas, you choose not to have the car the next night."

"That's a stupid rule, anyway."

"You're probably right."

Brandon's father realized that if he got angry with his son, the boy would focus his attention on the anger and not on his own responsibility in the situation. By using the parent talk *"You're probably right,"* he effectively took his sail out of his son's wind. With his sail down, the father could not be blown about by his son's bluster and posturing. By agreeing, *"You're probably right,"* he refused to get sucked into an argument, and he kept the conflict from escalating.

If you don't think this piece of parent talk will work with your children, you're probably right.

"Stop whining."

It is often necessary to send children verbal stop signs. There are times when we need them to stop hitting, tattling, putting someone down, or using inappropriate language. During those times, it is important to skillfully communicate our desire that a particular behavior end by using parent talk that is clear, direct, and effective.

Telling a child to "Stop whining," or "Stop calling your brother names," sends a red light signal that his current behavior needs to stop. While this style of parent talk sometimes produces short-term results, a different strategy is necessary to produce long-term behavior change. What is required is a clear communication that not only identifies the behavior that needs to be changed but suggests an alternative behavior to take the place of the undesirable one. For long-term effectiveness, *red light* parent talk needs a *green light* to accompany it.

The *red light/green light* Parent Talk System consists of two parts: the *red light* phase, which communicates "stop," and the *green light* phase, which teaches the new behavior or gives a "go." If you want your child to learn new behaviors that permanently replace the old ones, you need to arrange your language patterns to communicate both a *stop* and a *go*.

Effective red light language begins by calling the behavior by name.

> "John, that's name-calling."
> "Rebecca, that's tattling."
> "Tyrone, that's whining."

It is important that you call the behavior by the same name every time. It matters less what you call it and more that you stick with the name you decide upon for every occurrence. If you call the behavior whining one time, don't call it verbal manipulation later.

The second part of the red light phase communicates to the child that the behavior is inappropriate or doesn't work with you.

> "Whining doesn't work with me."
> "We don't allow put-downs in this family."
> "Hitting is not a behavior we use here."

Combine both parts of the red light phase to send a clear signal to the child to stop.

"John, that's name-calling. We voted at the family
meeting last week to eliminate that behavior."
"Tyrone, that's whining. Whining doesn't work
with me. I don't change my mind for people
who whine."
"Missy, that's hitting. We don't hit in this family."

Once again, always follow a red light with a green light.
The *go* step is where you teach the new behavior to tell your
child what *does* work with you.

"Please tell her what you want to have happen and
share how you're feeling."
"What works with me is if you ask in a normal voice.
Sometimes you get what you want and sometimes
you don't, but it's your only hope."
"Instead of tattling, please tell her directly."

When you use the *red light/green light* technique, the two
parts should flow together. Though they need to be thought
of as separate pieces, they are parts of a larger whole and need
to be delivered in one flowing communication.

"John, that's whining. Whining doesn't work with
me. I don't change my mind for people who whine.
What works with me is if you ask in a normal voice.
Sometimes you'll get what you want and sometimes
you won't, but it's your only hope."
"Mandy, that's name-calling. We don't do that in this

family. Please tell her directly what you want and
share how you are feeling."

When you use *red light/green light,* you teach your child
that she is only one choice away from getting what she wants
or from acting appropriately. When you teach her the new
behavior, you empower her to be able to make that choice
immediately. She is then more capable and more likely to
make the appropriate choice, now and in the future.

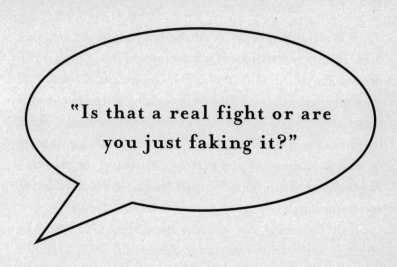

"Is that a real fight or are you just faking it?"

Dogs bark, cats meow, and children fight. You can count on it. Regardless of what you say, how you say it, or the alternatives you suggest, there will be fights among children in families, yours included. Simply stated, fights happen.

Fighting among children is a potentially dangerous situation. People can be injured. Feelings (as well as bodies) can be bruised. Both furniture and bones can be broken.

Sometimes fighting in families takes the form of imitating kung fu warriors, championship wrestlers, or hockey players releasing stress and tension. This kind of fighting can be characterized as play fighting and can be allowed as long as all parties buy into the fantasy.

Other times fights are real and need to be stopped immediately. Intervention is the appropriate parental action. Do it quickly and consistently.

When children begin to roughhouse, use parent talk that helps them stay conscious of whether or not the jostling is real or playful. Ask, *"Is this a real fight or are you just faking it?"* If necessary, remind them that play fighting is permitted; real fights are not. Use parent talk to reinforce the family norm that if both people don't agree to participate, the play fighting must stop: *"Remember, play fighting is by mutual consent only."* Play fighting that is not fun for all the parties involved has to end immediately.

If the fighting is real, you may not even need to ask. Take action at once, while using your parent talk skills. Describe what you see: *"I see two children who are furious and about to injure each other."* Describe the situation: *"This is not a good time for you to be together. You both need a time-out."* Describe the solution: *"I want both of you in your rooms, now. Let's go."*

Later, after an appropriate cooling-off period, you can lead the debriefing session. Feelings can be explored and validated. Solutions can be offered and evaluated. Decisions can be made and implemented. Healing can occur.

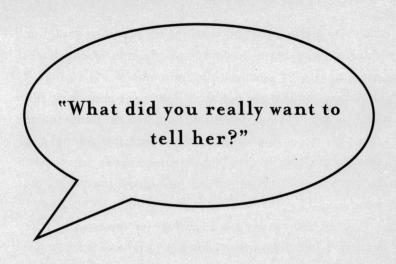

"What did you really want to tell her?"

"I think you're selfish."
"I hate you!"
"You stupid jerk."

Comments like these are delivered by children to children. They represent their best effort, under stress, to communicate with a sibling or friend. The communication is unhelpful because it escalates the conflict.

Parents who notice children using this nonproductive style of communication are faced with alternatives. They can launch into tirades on the evils of name-calling, they can use these opportunities to demonstrate problem solving, or they can explain to children the family rules on put-downs.

"What did you really want to tell her?" is my suggested

alternative. It asks the child uttering the put-down to stop and think. It forces her to become conscious and challenges her to get in touch with what it is she really wants.

Many children are not tuned in to the responsibility they have for getting what they want. They take the stance that the other person is responsible and choose name-calling in an attempt to change their sibling or friend. They give up their power by concentrating on the half of the interaction over which they have the least control.

When children are guided to discover and articulate their wants ("I don't like it when you put your foot on the rung of my chair"), they reclaim their personal power. They do so by choosing to focus on the responsibility *they* have to determine what happens.

Another drawback associated with name-calling is that it lets the other person off the hook. If children do not give clear, descriptive information about how and why they're reacting to another's behavior, they protect the other person from the necessity of looking at how his or her behavior affects others. When children call names, they give others a built-in excuse to get angry in return. The issue then becomes the name-calling rather than the precipitating behavior.

"What did you really want to tell her?" reminds children to determine what they want and to examine their language patterns to see if the two are congruent. Other parent talk that communicates the same message is:

"If you call her a name, she won't know why you're upset."
"What would you like her to do differently next time?"

"With all that name-calling, how did she know what
you wanted?"

Each is a variation of the *"What did you really want to tell
her?"* theme. Each is a way to help a child focus on her own
role in the interaction. Each helps the child become more self-
responsible.

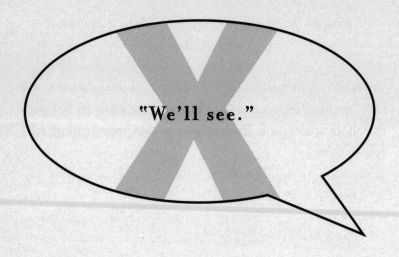

"We'll see."

"Can I spend the night at Martha's?"
"Will you take me to the mall later?"
"Can I have four friends sleep over for my birthday?"
"Would it be all right if I took the car Saturday afternoon?"
"How about treating me to the movies if I get an A on my
report card?"

To these questions and others like them, parents often respond
with "We'll see." *"We'll see"* is parent talk that removes an
immediate problem from our lives, delays it, and passes it on
to our children. The main issue for children concerning
"We'll see" is that it isn't an answer. To them it sounds and
feels more like a parental stalling tactic, and in many instances
that's exactly what it is.

   "We'll see" brings no closure. There is no resolution to the request, and the child is left wondering when and if a real answer will be forthcoming. Anxiety and feelings of power-lessness flow from the uncertainty of the situation and from her inability to do anything about obtaining a response.

When you can, use parent talk that immediately defines the situation. If your answer is no, say it promptly, with clar-ity and certainty. Don't use "We'll see" as the easy way out of a circumstance you don't want to face. If your answer is yes, let that word ring clear, as well.

On occasion, parents legitimately need time to ponder a child's request. If that's the case, it's appropriate to use parent talk that states your uncertainty and communicates an intent to give a definite answer at a later time.

"I'm not sure. Let me take some time to think about this. I'll let you know at dinner."
"I'll have to give this one some real thought. Check back with me right before bed and I'll give you my decision."
"That's the first time I've heard you ask that question. It's important that I think about it. I'll get back to you in an hour."

Stating a specific time when the answer will be delivered removes part of the doubt and uncertainty surrounding the request. Although children aren't sure at this point what your answer will be, at least they know when the decision will be announced. To build trust and strengthen your relationship, back up your parent talk with positive action by delivering your decision on schedule.

"My patience is running out."

Patience is often thought to be a characteristic of good teachers, parents, and even saints. It has long been considered a virtue. "She has the patience of Job." "She's so patient with those little children." "Oh, I admire your patience!"

I'd like to challenge the traditional point of view that patience is desirable, and encourage all parents to consider their use of this word. One dictionary defines *patient* as "bearing pains or trials calmly or without complaints; manifesting forbearance under provocation or strain; steadfast despite opposition, difficulty, or adversity." Another describes *patient* as "capable of bearing affliction with calmness."

The parent who understands the developmental capabilities of his child does not need to "bear pains calmly." He will accept behaviors that are developmentally appropriate and will not see the child as an adversary. The child will be viewed as innately good, though inexperienced. Parents who *under-stand* their children will see themselves as partners in learning and loving and will not view the child as "opposition." This adult will approach the child as a pleasure rather than as an adversary, a trial, or a difficulty.

An effective parent may not possess a great deal of patience, but he will understand children's needs and motivations. His virtue is not patience, because the grit-your-teeth-and-bear-it parent cannot be truly effective. His virtue is the behavior that flows from understanding that children need parents as guides and role models.

When you hear yourself say, "My patience is wearing thin; I'm getting impatient; my patience is running out," remind yourself that if you can *understand,* patience will be unnecessary. Use these words as a signal to question yourself. Ask, What is it here that I don't understand? Remind yourself, I'm not understanding this situation. Tell yourself, I don't understand this behavior. This will help you to consider other points of view. Pausing to remind yourself that patience indicates a lack of understanding will help you to move out of an emotional reaction and into an effective parenting stance.

While the patient adult is likely to see himself as a martyr, struggling through days of adversity imposed by his children, the understanding parent will celebrate *with* them the process of growth and development. The result will be increased enthusiasm and joy for all.

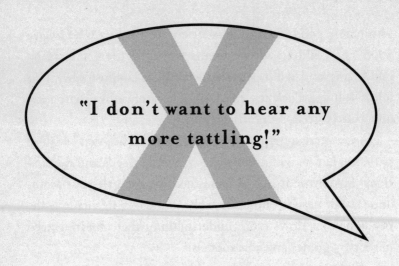

"I don't want to hear any more tattling!"

Grandma heard, "Susan threw sand!"
Father heard, "Bobby hit me!"
The fourth-grade teacher heard, "Joe looked at my paper!"
The bus driver heard, "He was poking me!"
All the adults replied, "I don't want to hear any more tattling!"

Children tattle. It matters very little whether or not adults want to hear it. They will. Count on it. Tattling is popular in the preschool and primary grades and continues through high school. Whatever the age of your child, you will hear tattling. Yet there are some strategies to help keep tattling and the accompanying irritation to a minimum.

The first helpful strategy is to increase your understanding. Tattling is called "prosocial aggression." It is a *natural* stage in the development of the conscience. It is a necessary and desirable, if somewhat unappealing, part of the developmental sequence. Once parents understand that tattling is normal and inevitable, they'll be less likely to resent it and more likely to deal with it effectively.

Sometimes we reinforce tattling because we need to hear about a situation. If Cindy is stuck in a tree or Terry has hurt himself, you want to know. Because you respond, even though it's out of necessity, the tattling is reinforced. At other times, you don't need or want the information supplied by tattling. If Cindy was reprimanded by her soccer coach or if Terry stayed on the phone three minutes over his limit, you do not necessarily want to know. This tattling springs from a desire to get another child in trouble rather than from a wish to be helpful.

It's because some tattling is helpful and other expressions of it are not that children are apt to overuse it. They don't understand that situations differ, and they must be encouraged to consider more than one aspect of any circumstance. The positive intentions of gaining recognition from the parent or other adult and of having some control preempt other considerations. I suggest that you ask the tattling child, *"Is this helpful or unhelpful?"* This parent talk forces her into a decision-making mode and requires that she do a bit of mental work: deciding, discriminating, problem solving. *"Is this helpful or unhelpful?"* encourages the child to move the focus from fixing blame and getting someone else in trouble to the decision that is required.

Once the child decides whether her tattling is helpful or unhelpful, let her know that you're interested only in helpful information. This encourages a cooperative home environment, since children learn the difference between "tattling" and telling. They learn quickly that your interest lies in helping family members to support one another rather than on affixing blame.

Another parent talk strategy that discourages tattling is to instruct the tattling child to settle the problem with words. Say *"If you don't like it, tell him not to hit you. Say that you don't like fighting."* This language technique moves the responsibility for solving the problem from the parent to the tattling child. It demonstrates your trust in and respect of her ability to take care of herself.

Encouraging students to settle problems with words, or asking them, *"Is this helpful or unhelpful?"* keeps the parent from having to pass judgment on something that he has not seen. It is risky to make decisions, affix blame, or discipline children based on the hearsay of other children. The story you hear may or may not resemble what really happened. Each person's view of reality is greatly influenced by her own needs and desires.

Children will tattle. Until you accept that fact, you may feel impatience and frustration. I suggest that you relax, accept tattling as normal and inevitable, and lean into it. Enjoy it as an opportunity to use your new parent talk language skills and move your children beyond tattling to a new level of self-responsibility.

Odds and Ends

"I'm proud for you."

Participants who attend my Parent Talk seminars are often surprised to hear some of my language recommendations. At no time, however, do their faces reveal greater surprise than when I suggest they drop "I'm proud of you" from their verbal repertoire. What can be wrong with this one? they wonder.

I believe that "I'm proud of you" is condescending. The speaker takes the role of evaluator and assumes the right to judge the accomplishment of the person who achieved it. The judge looks down and pronounces, "I'm proud of you." This language gives us the image of the master patting a well-behaved puppy on the head.

You can strengthen the phrase "I'm proud of you" and create the positive effects you intend by changing one word. Replace *of* with *for*. Instead of "I'm proud of you," the statement becomes "I'm proud *for* you."

Say this revised phrase out loud. *"I'm proud for you."* Hear the subtle difference. You may want to practice this one aloud several times while alternating *of* and *for*. Tune in to your feelings as you speak.

"I'm proud *for* you" keeps the focus on the doer. The speaker appreciates and communicates pleasure in the other person's accomplishment. Attention and credit go to the doer.

Imagine that you wrote me a letter detailing your reaction to one of my parent presentations. Think about how you would choose to feel as you read my letter of response informing you that I was very proud of your ability to articulate your thoughts. "Who is he to judge *me?*" might be your reaction. Indeed, who am I to be proud of *you?* It is up to you to be proud of you if you choose, for reasons you alone determine.

> "Chad, your coat is on the floor. I'm getting angry. It belongs on a hanger in the closet."

Jerrod's mother noticed his brand-new baseball glove laying outside in the rain. She was tempted to vent her frustration with words that scolded. Instead, she replied, *"I see your new glove getting soaked in the rain. I feel frustrated. Ball gloves belong in the sports box."* Jerrod immediately brought it inside.

Felicia's father felt his irritation kick in when he saw the library books scattered on the floor. He wanted to give one of his eloquent lectures about respect for materials. He resisted his urge to launch into a verbalization full of reasons, consequences, and responsibilities and chose to say instead, *"The library books are on the floor. I'm feeling irritated. They belong on the shelf."* Felicia and her sister responded with the desired behavior and returned the books to the shelf.

Chad's coat was once again left in a heap on the floor by the top of the basement stairs. His mother wanted to remind him again of the number of times she had reminded him already. She didn't. She chose parent talk that stated, *"Chad, your coat is on the floor. I'm getting angry. It belongs on a hanger in the closet."* Hearing his mom's request, Chad reacted favorably and hung it up.

Each of these parents was successful in obtaining the behavior they desired. Each was equally successful in using an important parent talk strategy, the *"describe, describe, describe"* technique. They described what they saw. They described what they felt. And they described what needed to be done.

By focusing your parent talk on descriptions, you keep yourself from pointing accusing fingers or attacking the child's personality. It helps you assume an important stance, that of speaking to the situation rather than to the character or personality of the child.

"I see your brand-new baseball glove getting soaked in the rain" describes the situation. This style of speaking is preferable to "Why can't you ever remember to bring in your ball glove?" The latter attacks the character of the person responsible. *"The library books are on the floor"* speaks to the situation at hand, while "Can't you be more respectful than that with books that belong to someone else?" points to the child's personality.

"I'm getting angry" and *"I feel frustrated"* describe how the parent is feeling. Children deserve to get clear messages of parental feelings. That is done best by wrapping your feelings in descriptive rather than accusatory language. To do this effectively, concentrate on describing how you feel.

"Your coat belongs on a hanger in the closet" describes what needs to be done. So does *"Books belong on the shelf."* When

your language concentrates on what needs to be done, you are again speaking to the situation. Your language points to the solution rather than to the person who created the problem.

When tempted to belittle, get after, lecture, or scold, remember to *describe, describe, describe*. Describe what you see: *"I see dirty dishes on the dinner table."* Describe your feelings: *"I feel irritated."* Describe what needs to be done: *"The dishes need to be rinsed off and placed in the dishwasher."*

The *describe, describe, describe* technique is no guarantee that your child's behavior will match your desires. It is certain, though, that your words will refrain from attacking personality or character. It will mean that your language shows the respect you hope to elicit from the receiver. And it will mean that you are becoming increasingly skilled at nonjudgmental, healthy parent talk.

> **"Luis, as you hang up your coat, please straighten the boots in the closet."**

"Austin, while you put your bike away, just put those two
tools back on the table, please."
"Chelsea, as you bring the groceries in from the car, please
pick up the litter on the front seat."

These examples of parent talk employ a strategy called the
double task assignment. Assigning tasks that are linked is usually more effective than assigning each separately. When you
say, *"Leslie, as you get those dirty dishes from your room, please
put these towels in the upstairs closet,"* your parent talk has the
sound of a single task. Since two tasks are combined in your
sentence, it has the effect of making the task appear easier and
quicker.

When you ask that the dirty dishes be returned and then
ask that the towels be put away, you make the tasks appear

bigger and more difficult. With the tasks divided, it is easier to refuse one or the other. Linking them through your parent talk makes refusal more difficult because the child has to expend effort to determine which one of the tasks she is refusing. Having to engage in that thinking process often serves as a deterrent to youngsters who find it easier to just perform the tasks than think about them.

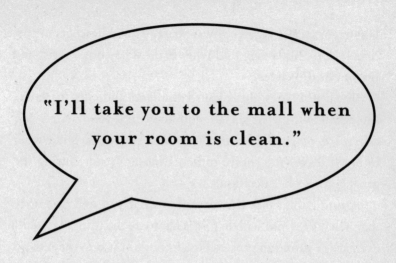

"I'll take you to the mall when your room is clean."

"I'll drive you to soccer when the grass is cut."
"I'll be glad to listen to your concerns when you speak to
me in a normal voice."

These examples of parent talk are effective because they inform the child what *you* will do. They focus on the piece of the equation over which you have control. You are in charge of you. You control your own reactions and behaviors. You get to decide what *you* do. Your words describe something you can enforce, *your* behavior.

Using parent talk that tells a child what *you* will do is more effective than telling her what *she* will do.

"Cut the lawn now" or "Clean up your room this minute" focus on what the *child* is to do. Not only do you have less control over what *she* does than over what *you* do, but this style of language often instigates power struggles. Adolescents in particular don't like being told what to do. They often resist and resent our directives.

Even if a child obeys your command and cuts the lawn, she is following *your* dictate and activating *your* desire. *"I'll take you to the mall when the grass is cut,"* doesn't tell her what to do. It leaves the choice to her. Cutting or not cutting the grass becomes her decision.

Using parent talk that describes what you will do rather than what the child will do forces her to do the thinking. Children are required to process how important it is to them to go to the mall, attend the soccer game, or have you listen to their concerns. They weigh the alternatives and decide for themselves. This inner thinking and choice making on their part results in less resistance, less resentment, and less hassle.

When you use parent talk that speaks to what you *will* do rather than to what you *won't* do, you'll get more positive results. *"I'll unlock the Sega Genesis when the family room is cleaned up"* gets more cooperation than "I won't unlock the Sega Genesis until the family room is cleaned up." *"I'll serve dinner as soon as I get help setting the table"* is more effective than "I won't serve dinner until I get help setting the table."

Use positive phrasing that informs your child what *you* will do and enjoy the benefits of her increased cooperation and self-responsibility.

"MY LIFE'S BEEN A LOT EASIER AROUND HERE SINCE I HID MY MOM'S *PARENT TALK* BOOK."

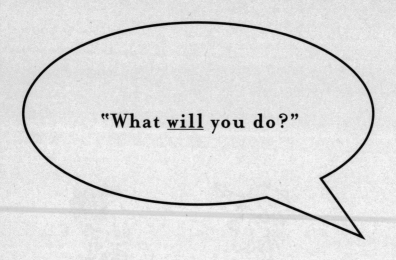

"What <u>will</u> you do?"

Each of the following statements represents a child's honest desire to change an undesirable behavior.

"I won't hit him anymore."
"I won't be late again."
"I won't forget to give it to him."

Parents can help turn these positive *intentions* into positive *actions* by inviting children to think about and articulate alternative behaviors. Ask them, *"What* will *you do?"* This question moves children's thinking from what they will *not* do (hitting, arriving late, or forgetting) to what they *will* do instead.

"I won't hit him anymore" or "I won't be late again" are easy answers that children feed us to get themselves off the hook. The phrase *"What* will *you do?"* forces them to pause and think about positive behaviors. It shifts their attention from the easy "won't do" statements to more serious thought about helpful alternatives.

"What will *you do?"* is an invitation to articulate a plan of action that focuses on the positive. By stating that plan aloud, the child's commitment is strengthened and he is more likely to put his plan into action.

"What will *you do?"* is a helpful question to ask *yourself* as you implement the ideas in this piece. When you seem to be stuck in old language patterns that no longer feel comfortable, use the question to clarify your thoughts and intentions. Your language will change as you focus on defining what you *will* do.

"I love you, and I don't like that behavior."

Children often choose behaviors we don't appreciate. They act in ways we don't condone. And they pick actions that aren't appropriate. It is during these difficult moments that our parent talk must demonstrate an important principle: *Separate the deed from the doer.*

> "I like you Sarah, but I don't shop with people who choose that behavior."
> "Jacob, I love you, but when you hit your sister you choose time-out."
> "Larry, I really enjoy being with you, but when you decide to be that loud I need to be somewhere else."

This kind of language makes it clear that although the parent does not enjoy or must limit the behavior, she still likes the child. It is not the child who is disapproved of. It is the behavior.

Some children think they *are* their behavior. They equate *themselves* with their actions. Children are not their report card. They are not whether or not they made the team or got picked for first chair or fifth chair in band. They are not the language they chose to use at Grandma's. Nor are they the tantrum they threw in the shoe store.

Children are much more than their behavior. They are creations of God, filled with light and love. A temper tantrum isn't their essence. Neither is whining or lying. These temporary behaviors aren't who they really are. They're simple manifestations of the act they are choosing at this moment. Love is still their essential ingredient. If we don't help our children appreciate that notion, who will?

Spiritually, the concept is stated this way: Hate the sin, love the sinner. When you choose language that separates the deed from the doer, you put this universal spiritual practice to use in your own family.

"Robin, you have two choices. You can stop that behavior and we'll stay and shop, or you can continue that behavior and we'll go home. It's up to you. And Robin, I like you a whole bunch. It's just that I don't shop with people who beg like that. If I took Grandma shopping and she begged and begged, we'd go home. See, it's not you. It's the behavior I don't enjoy."

Help your child realize she is not her behavior. When disciplining, choose parent talk that drives a wedge between the deed and the doer.

"I'm really surprised."

"What a shock!"
"I can hardly believe this."
"This takes me by surprise."
"I sure didn't expect this."
"This catches me off guard."

Surprise talk is a language technique that can be used to communicate positive expectations to your children. Use it immediately following a behavior you find inappropriate. When your child brings home an inadequate report card, remark, *"This sure is a surprise."* If your son is asked to stay after school to make up work, let your initial reaction be *"This is hard to believe."* If your daughter is suspended from her softball team for insubordination, say *"This has really taken me by surprise!"*

When you use surprise talk, the message you send communicates much more than surprise. The real message is: I didn't expect this. I don't see you this way. This behavior doesn't fit with my picture of you. The way I hold you in my consciousness is a lot different than this. This kind of parent talk informs your child that, in your mind, this particular behavior is not who and what they really are.

"Well, I'm not surprised" is language that announces to the child that the behavior was expected. "I would have predicted this," following a suspension; "No shock here," after examining a poor report card; and "Just about what I expected," at the conclusion of a below-standard effort at mowing the grass invite the same behaviors in the future. After all, as evidenced by your parent talk, the behaviors were, and still are, expected.

Be careful how you react to your children's successes. Following a positive musical performance, *"What a surprise"* informs the child that his behavior was not expected. "A real shocker," at the conclusion of your daughter's two-home-run effort, tells her you don't believe it could happen again. "This is hard to believe," when it follows an A on a school project, is not a compliment. It is language that says, "I don't see you as being this capable."

Expect the best from your children, knowing that their behaviors will not always match your high expectations. If a particular behavior is disappointing, act and sound surprised. The results you get could be a pleasant surprise.

"It's homework time."

Misty's parents believe in encouraging her to do well in school. They attend parent-teacher conferences, show interest in her papers and report card, and do their best to help her if she gets stuck with homework. They even have a special time, between 7:00 and 8:00 p.m., that is set aside as *homework time.*

Each evening, as 7:00 p.m. arrives, Misty's dad announces, "It's homework time," and begins what all too often erupts into a full-blown argument. A typical conversation follows:

"It's homework time."
"I don't have any homework."
"What do you mean, you don't have any homework?"
"I don't have any. I got it all done at school."
"Then how come you brought books home in your backpack?"

"I didn't want to go all the way back to my locker after
my last class."
"What about history?"
"She didn't assign anything today. She gave
us a break."
*"Are you sure you don't have homework? What about
math? Did you get that all done?"*
"Yes, I got my math done. We didn't have as much
as we usually do."
"Let me see it."
"Dad, I got it done at school and left it there. Don't
you believe me?"
"I have a tough time believing you don't have any homework."
"Well, I don't."

Such hassles over homework time could be significantly reduced with a slight adjustment in the parent talk
used. Change the words and the concept of *homework* time
to *study time*. When your parent talk becomes, "It's *study*
time," the response, "I don't have any homework," takes
on new meaning. A child doesn't need homework to
engage in study. She can reread a chapter, look up vocabulary used in the chapter, review her notes, study for a test,
or read supplemental material. Massive studying can go on
without one piece of homework that needs to be turned in
the next day.

"It's homework time"creates the impression that the time
allotted is for homework, and since the child has no homework, she can choose other activities during that time. "It's
study time" implies that this is school-related time only, a time

to do homework, review, study, or read for further information.

Reduce schoolwork confrontation in your family by changing your parent talk and the notion of *homework* time to *study* time.

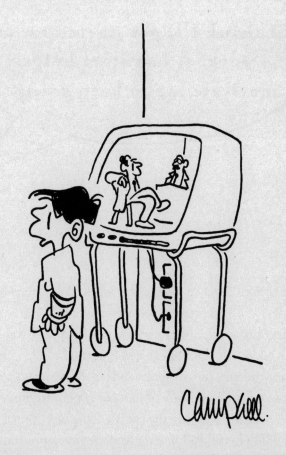

"HEY, MOM! THIS GUY SAYS HE'S ON THE SHOW TO PLUG HIS PARENT TALK BOOK. WHAT'S A BOOK?"

> **"I think I'll get started on my work. A fast start helps motivate me to keep going."**

"I think I'll get started on my work. A fast start helps motivate me to keep going."

"I'm going to take just an average helping. If I want more later, I can always get it."

"I enjoy the way the car looks and smells when it's clean. I'm going to give myself some of that enjoyment right now. I'll be outside washing the car if anyone needs me."

"I'm going to call Bill. I want to share my appreciation with him about the effort he put in on our new project this week."

Self-referred comments such as these are one useful way to communicate your values, ideals, and personal standards to your children. To make a self-referred comment, structure the first part of your parent talk so that you are speaking about yourself.

"I think I'll organize the garage."
"I'm going to get on my treadmill now."
"I'll pass on the candy, thanks."
"I'm going to get dressed for church now."

Follow your statement about yourself with a values connection.

"It's so much easier to find things when the garage
is organized."
"My body deserves this regular workout."
"I want nutritious foods filling my engine."
"Singing those hymns and praying with others helps me
feel connected to the Lord."

Attitudes are more easily caught than taught. Modeling organization, appreciation, regular exercise, healthy eating, and getting started quickly is more effective than the most eloquent of lectures. Children are notorious for letting our best mini-speeches go in one ear and out the other. It's called being open-minded. When we walk our talk by living our values, the intended message is more likely to register.

To increase the chances that your modeling is noticed and processed, use self-referred statements to talk about it as you do it. Adding verbal comments to your behaviors combines auditory and visual learning components. Used together, the two modes create greater impact in your child's heart and mind than would be the case if they were used independently. Announce *"I always feel better when my chores are done. I think I'll do those first today,"* then give support to your parent talk by following through. Pause as you finish this section of *Parent Talk* and let your children overhear you say, *"I gain so much information and so many useful ideas from reading. I just love this book."* Then let them see you continue to read for the next few minutes. Say *"Boy, I enjoy reading,"* as you bookmark your page and put the book away.

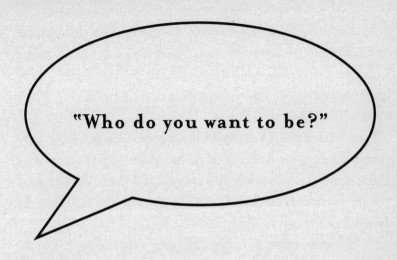

"Who do you want to be?"

Take care not to confuse this important piece of parent talk with the often asked question *"What* do you want to be?" The *what* question is about career choices, job opportunities, and occupational preferences. Although "What do you want to be?" is a useful query to make of a child at any age, it is vastly different from the question that heads this section.

"Who do you want to be?" is about values. It is about choosing who we are in relation to the events and circumstances that surround us. Deciding who we are is a process that goes on our entire lives. We create who we want to be by how we choose to respond to the situations in our lives. All of us, including our children, define and redefine who we are daily, without giving the process much thought. *"Who do you want to be?"* is a question that invites our children to think seriously about who they really are.

Use *"Who do you want to be?"* to respond to a child facing a dilemma.

Example 1

"Dad, what should I do about the school election? Most people are voting for Roger because he's popular and an athlete. Jake wants me to work on his campaign. I think he'd make a better president, but my friends might not like it. What do you think I ought to do?"

"Christine, what choice feels like who you really are? Who do you want to be in this situation?"

Example 2

"Mom, Butch didn't get invited to Ed's party. I feel really bad for him. Do you think I ought to stay home and do something with him?"

"Who do you want to be in this case, Jerry? Which choice feels like who you really are?"

Helping our children decide who they are and who they want to be in their lives is one of our most important roles. It is not our job to decide for our children, but it is our responsibility to help them stay awake regarding the decisions they make on this issue. Asking them occasionally *"Who do you want to be here?"* increases the chance that they will make conscious choices in this area.

Hardships enter our lives to help us decide who we want to be in relation to those situations. Likewise, pleasant events arrive to help us decide who we really are with respect to those circumstances. Acquaintances, coworkers, neighbors, and our children also appear in our lives to help us decide who we want to be in the context of those relationships.

Think about this issue as it applies to you for a moment. When a child comes to you with a concern, problem, or tough decision, she is presenting you with an opportunity to decide who *you* want to be in that situation. You can decide to be a parent who tells your child what to do, imposing your interpretations of right and wrong on her. Or you can ask, *"Who do you want to be in this situation?"* The latter response encourages the child to think through the decision and its possible consequences and helps her create an internal standard to carry with her wherever she goes.

Parenting gives us numerous opportunities to create who we want to be within the parenting role. Who *you* want to be could well be someone who asks children, *"Who do you want to be?"*

"I love you."

There is only one parent talk phrase that appears more than once in this book. This is it. That *"I love you"* is included a second time pays tribute to its importance and reaffirms the need for the phrase to be spoken frequently by parents to their children, as well as to each other.

"Dad, it's Jenny. Call me right away as soon as you get this message. Something terrible has happened. I'm okay, but I have to talk to you." This message is word-for-word as I heard it on my answering machine one July morning. July 9, 1997, to be exact. I can put my daughter's words on paper, but the tone and the chill they produced in my stomach cannot be captured here. The return call to Jenny delivered the information no parent ever expects or wants to hear. My oldest boy, Randy, was dead.

Randy died a month short of his thirtieth birthday, so he

wasn't really a boy. He was a grown man. Except that he was *my* boy. Children never stop being your children. It doesn't matter how old they are. And now my son was dead. With no warning, with no chance to say good-bye, Randy was gone.

Comfort came and continues to arrive in a variety of shapes and forms. Friends and relatives have been there when I needed them with kind words, reassurance, and a listening ear. Friends at my country dance club presented me with an engraved belt buckle in Randy's memory. The right book appeared at the right time. My faith that the soul endures into eternity has been reinforced and affirmed. God has invited me again to relax into the presence of His unconditional love.

Our family rallied together. We give each other love and support, hugs and listening, time and caring. We connect for and with each other.

I think of Randy every day. I miss him. Mostly I remember the happy times. I taught him to hit a baseball, you know. He made me pitch to him for hours. He pitched a no-hitter once in Little League. I remember the pride he felt the day he beat me in a ten-kilometer race and the grin he had on his face when he moved past me on Heartbreak Hill, across from the YMCA in Kalamazoo, Michigan. He never looked back, but I knew he was smiling the satisfaction of a young man who had just completed a rite of passage. I never enjoyed losing more. I was there when he learned to ride a bike. I remember his first car, big and ugly. A gas guzzler. Randy loved it.

I have many positive memories of my son and of our time together. But there is one memory that is more important to me than all the others. It is the one that sustains me and gives me comfort when I reenter the grieving process. It is the one

I hang on to whenever I feel sad or reflect on Randy's death. It is the one I cannot imagine doing without. It is the memory of our last conversation.

No, I don't know what we talked about that day on the phone. Michigan football probably. Or maybe the Bears or the Buccaneers. The guts of the conversation doesn't matter, only the ending. You know what it was.

"I love you, Son."

"I love you, too, Dad."

About Chick Moorman

Chick Moorman is an inspirational speaker who has addressed more than 300,000 parents and educators while conducting more than 2,000 talks on raising and educating responsible children. He is a former classroom teacher with more than thirty-five years of experience in the field of education. His mission is to empower teachers and parents so they can in turn empower others. He resides in Merrill, Michigan, where he relaxes by riding Arabian horses. Contact him, toll free, at 877-360-1477, e-mail him at ipp57@aol.com, or visit his web site, www.chickmoorman.com.

Training, Seminars, and Workshops

Chick Moorman conducts full-day workshops for school districts and parent groups. He also delivers keynote addresses for local, state, and national conferences.

For Educators

Achievement Motivation and Behavior Management (Teacher Talk)
Teaching for Respect and Responsibility
Celebrate the Spirit Whisperers

For Parents

Parent Talk: Words That Empower, Words That Wound
Raising Response-Able Children
The Language of Response-Able Parenting

Parent Talk Facilitator Training

The facilitator training is designed to prepare local trainers to skillfully present the Parent Talk System to parents in their communities. This three-day training will help you teach parents how to raise responsible children. Includes techniques to assist parents to learn communication strategies to build love, trust, and mutual respect within their families. Participants learn training strategies that allow them to teach the Parent Talk System with expertise and confidence.

When you become a Parent Talk System facilitator, you will join a select group of people throughout the world who are already working to use these skills to improve family life in their communities. Information on the next facilitator training can be obtained by e-mailing ipp57@aol.com or calling toll free, 877-360-1477.

Books

Teacher Talk: What It Really Means (Chick Moorman and Nancy Weber)
Talk Sense To Yourself: The Language of Personal Power
Spirit Whisperers: Teachers Who Nourish a Child's Spirit

Our Classroom: We Can Learn Together (Chick Moorman
   and Dee Dishon)

Where the Heart Is: Stories of Home and Family

Other Products

Parent Talk Focus Cards (card deck)

The Language of Response-Able Parenting (five–cassette
   tape series)

Reducing Family Conflict Through Effective Parent Talk
   (video)

The Parent Talk System Facilitator's Manual (training
   manual)

> **Ordering information is available at**
> **www.chickmoorman.com or toll free, 877-360-1477.**